IN THE LINE OF FIRE

IN THE LINE OF FIRE

Presidents' Lives at Stake

by Judith St. George

SCHOLASTIC INC.

New York   Toronto   London   Auckland   Sydney
Mexico City   New Delhi   Hong Kong

ISBN 0-439-28318-3

12 11 10 9 8 7 6 5 4 3 2 1   1 2 3 4 5 6/0

Printed in the U.S.A.   14

First Scholastic printing, October 2001

To David

Contents

INTRODUCTION

The inauguration of a new president is traditionally a festive celebration. The outgoing and incoming presidents drive to the Capitol together for the swearing-in ceremony. They smile, wave to the crowds, and at least appear to be cordial to each other.

Yet the changeover of presidents hasn't always been festive. Since 1865 four stunned and somber vice-presidents have taken the oath of office after the assassination of a president. There have been seven other assassination attempts, putting the lives of some twenty-five percent of American presidents at stake. The presidency is a dangerous job.

The word *assassin* comes from the twelfth-century Arabic word *hashshash*, meaning "hashish smoker." A ruthless sect of Muslims, who ate or smoked the drug hashish, committed cold-blooded murder solely for political reasons. American presidential assassinations and attempted assassinations have been committed the same way, ruthlessly and in cold blood.

Even though the details of the assassinations differ, for the purpose of this book, each story is divided into four sections. The first section focuses on the president, his background, character, politics, and especially the circumstances of his death. The second section concerns the assassin or assassins. Who committed this terrible deed, and why? The newly sworn-in president's policies and goals make up the third part. Last is the impact that the assassinations had on the nation. A final chapter briefly relates the seven assassination attempts.

These stories are tragic stories, but in a sense, they are also triumphant stories. Although the assassination of a leader often brings down governments in other countries, that has never happened in the United States. The Constitution safeguards the office of the presidency.

The Constitution states: "In Case of the Removal of the President from Office, or of his Death, Resignation, or Inability to discharge the Powers and Duties of the said Office, the same shall devolve on the Vice President."

Shock, outrage, and grief have always followed the assassination of a president. But after Americans have mourned and honored their martyred president, they have rallied to move forward into the future under their new leader.

IN THE LINE OF FIRE

APRIL 14, 1865

On the afternoon of April 14, the president and his wife went for a carriage ride. They rode out to the Navy Yard, where the president chatted with some sailors and toured a ship, the Montauk. "Dear Husband, you almost startle me by your great cheerfulness," the First Lady said with a smile.

By late in the day both the president's mood and the weather had darkened. In a talk with his bodyguard, the president said: "Crook, do you know, I believe there are men who want to take my life." He added, "I know no one could do it and escape alive. But if it is to be done, it is impossible to prevent."

It didn't help the president's mood that their guests for the evening had sent their regrets. Everyone else the president and First Lady invited had also politely declined. The First Lady suggested that perhaps they should stay home, instead of going out. The president objected. The newspapers had already announced their plans and he didn't want to disappoint the public. Finally, a young Washington couple accepted their invitation.

That evening, the president and his wife were late leaving the White House to pick up their guests. They were just stepping into their carriage when a caller arrived. "Excuse me now," the president told him. "I am going to the theatre. Come and see me in the morning."

"WHO IS DEAD IN THE WHITE HOUSE?"

ABRAHAM LINCOLN
February 12, 1809–April 15, 1865
Sixteenth President, 1861–1865

FORD'S THEATRE

President Abraham Lincoln, his wife, Mary, and their guests, Clara Harris and her fiancé, Major Henry Rathbone, arrived at Ford's Theatre a half hour late. The play had already begun, but when the Lincolns approached the state box, the actors paused and the orchestra struck up "Hail to the Chief." Even though it was Good Friday, the theater was nearly full. Many of the seventeen hundred playgoers had come because they had read in the newspapers that the president would be there. They greeted the Lincolns with cheers and applause.

The audience was in a festive mood. Five days before, Confederate General Robert E. Lee had surrendered to Union Army General Ulysses S. Grant. Although some fighting still continued, for all intents and purposes, the Civil War was over. With more than 600,000 American lives lost, the past four years had seen little laughter.

Now the audience at Ford's Theatre was ready to enjoy a silly play called *Our American Cousin*. Mrs. Lincoln was all smiles as her party entered the flag-draped state box. The president, who looked tired and serious, simply raised his hand and bowed.

To provide a comfortable setting, the theater management had combined two boxes overlooking the stage and brought in special furniture. Lincoln seated himself toward the back in a rocking chair. Mrs. Lincoln took the chair beside him. Miss Harris sat on the Lincolns' right, with Major Rathbone seated on the sofa next to her.

As the play continued, Mrs. Lincoln laughed heartily. She moved closer to her husband and put her hand on his knee. "What will Miss Harris think of my hanging on to you so?" she asked in a whisper.

Lincoln smiled. "She won't think anything about it," he replied.

More than twenty years had passed since Abraham Lincoln and Mary Todd were married in Springfield, Illinois, on November 4, 1842. Although Mary Lincoln was emotionally unstable and the marriage had its stormy moments, the Lincolns loved each another. And they adored their four sons, Robert Todd, Edward Baker, William Wallace, and Thomas, known as Tad.

Tragically, four-year-old Eddie died in 1850. Twelve years later, the Lincolns' son Willie died in the White House at the age of eleven. The death of their two sons and four cruel years of war had taken their toll on Abraham Lincoln. At fifty-six, his face was etched with lines, and he looked older than his years.

Now the president's face was hidden from the audience by a curtain. It was impossible for the theatergoers to see whether he was enjoying the play or not. At one point he felt chilly and got up to put on his overcoat.

The third act had already begun when the door to the state box opened silently. A man holding a small derringer pistol in one hand and a dagger in the other stepped inside. He stood directly behind the president, whose back was to the door. The man raised his pistol and fired. A large hand-made lead bullet struck Abraham Lincoln behind his left ear, passed through his skull into his brain, and came to rest behind his right eye.

For a moment no one moved as smoke enveloped the president. Then, as he slumped forward, Mrs. Lincoln reached out and grabbed him. At the same time, Major Rathbone sprang to his feet and lunged at the gunman. Dropping his pistol, the man slashed Rathbone's left arm to the bone with his dagger.

As the wounded Rathbone tried to stop him, the man vaulted over the railing and leapt more than eleven feet onto the stage. He fell heavily on one foot. Still holding his dagger, he pulled himself upright. Some people heard the man shout: "Sic semper tyrannis!" It was Virginia's state motto, "Thus always to tyrants!" With that, he fled backstage.

Many in the audience recognized the man. He was a promising young actor, John Wilkes Booth. What was going on? Was this part of the play? Then Major Rathbone leaned over the railing. "Stop that man!" he yelled.

"They have shot the president! They have shot the president!" came a scream from the state box.

People jumped up in horror and spilled into the aisles.

"A surgeon! A surgeon!" a voice shouted.

No one was aware that an armed man had entered the president's box until the fatal shot was fired.

Other voices called out: "Hang him! Kill him!"

Clara Harris cried out for someone to bring water.

A young army doctor, Charles Leale, was the first to enter the state box. Mrs. Lincoln was still holding on to the president. "Oh, Doctor, do what you can for my dear husband," she sobbed. "Is he dead? Can he recover?"

Dr. Leale laid Lincoln on the floor and quickly examined him. The injury was grave. He cut away Lincoln's collar and coat and removed a blood clot from the wound to relieve the pressure. The president's breathing eased slightly. A second army doctor was lifted from the stage into the box. As soldiers began to clear the near-rioting audience from the theater, two more doctors appeared. The four men worked frantically to revive the president.

Dr. Leale pronounced the president's fate, "His wound is mortal. It is impossible for him to recover."

Everyone's worst nightmare had come to pass. Lincoln had been warned over and over to avoid crowds. Only a few days before, his friend and sometime bodyguard, Ward Hill Lamon, had left Washington on a government errand. "Promise me you will not go out at night while I am gone, particularly to the theater," Lamon had warned. Secretary of War Edwin Stanton had earlier refused the Lincolns' theater invitation hoping that the president wouldn't go either.

Even before he took office, Lincoln had received death threats. As he traveled to Washington for his 1861 inauguration, an assassination plot had surfaced in Baltimore. Disguised in a short coat, felt hat, and long muffler, Lincoln had secretly changed trains in Philadelphia. He had arrived in Washington unannounced…and safe.

Once Lincoln was president, hate mail flooded the White House. Most, but not all, was from Southerners. Nevertheless, the president refused to have uniformed guards at the White House and often slipped out to walk the streets alone, even at night.

As the war dragged on, death and kidnapping threats increased. Whether Lincoln liked it or not, security was stepped up. A cavalry company escorted the Lincolns to and from their summer cottage at the Soldiers' Home in northwest Washington. Guards were posted at the White House gates and front portico. Armed Metropolitan policemen in plain clothes accompanied the president at all times. A policeman was on duty every night outside the Lincolns' private rooms.

Despite the added protection, someone fired a shot at Lincoln while he was riding horseback alone on the night of September 26, 1864. The next day, one of his guards found a bullet hole in the crown of the president's stovepipe hat.

The president was well aware that he was at risk. He once showed a reporter a pile of eighty menacing letters in his desk. "I know I am in danger," he said, "but I am not going to worry over threats like these."

But Lincoln wasn't able to dismiss thoughts of assassination completely. Only weeks before he was shot, he had told Ward Hill Lamon about a dream he'd had. The president dreamed that he heard sobbing in the White House. He followed the crying to the East Room, where he saw a corpse resting on a platform draped in black. The platform, called a catafalque, was surrounded by people weeping. "Who is dead in the White House?" he asked a soldier. "The president," came the answer. "He was killed by an assassin!" Lincoln admitted that he slept no more that night.

Lincoln's bodyguard, William Crook, never forgot the president's parting words as he left for Ford's Theatre. Instead of his usual "Good night, Crook," Lincoln had said, "Good-bye, Crook."

Although William Crook often accompanied the president to the theater, for some unknown reason, John Parker of the Metropolitan Police had been assigned to the Lincolns for the evening. Parker had a poor performance record and had been charged twice by the police board for neglecting his duty. At Ford's Theatre Parker once again neglected his duty. Deserting his post outside the state box, he watched the play briefly and then joined friends for a drink. The president was left unguarded. The assassin entered the box. The fatal shot was fired.

As the president lay mortally wounded, someone suggested that he be taken back to the White House. Dr. Leale refused, knowing that Lincoln would not survive the ride over Washington's bumpy cobblestone streets. "We must get him to the nearest bed," he ordered.

With Mrs. Lincoln continuing to sob loudly, the four doctors carefully lifted the unconscious president. Other men volunteered their help. Armed soldiers held back the frenzied crowds as Lincoln was carried across Tenth Street to a house owned by William Petersen. He was taken up the front steps, down the hall, and into a small back bedroom. Because the mattress was too short for Lincoln's six-foot-four-inch frame, he was laid across the bed diagonally.

Mary Lincoln's voice was heard in the hallway. "Where is my dear husband? Where is he?" she cried. She appeared in the doorway, her skirts and shoes muddy from crossing Tenth Street. The doctors, who were about to examine Lincoln, asked her to leave. A front parlor became her headquarters for the night.

Abraham Lincoln's image grew even taller after he won the 1864 election.

Twenty-one-year-old Robert Lincoln was summoned. For the rest of his life, Robert would regret that he had turned down his parents' invitation to join them at Ford's Theatre. He could do nothing to help his father now but stand and watch as nearly a dozen doctors kept up their efforts to do something, anything.

All sorts of people drifted in and out of the little back room: cabinet members, senators, congressmen, Lincoln's minister, friends, actors, even curious bystanders. This was the president of the United States who had been shot! This was the man who had saved their nation!

Considering his background, the likelihood that Abraham Lincoln would have ever attained the presidency seemed remote, if not impossible. Born to poverty on February 12, 1809, in a one-room Kentucky log cabin, young Abe lost his mother when he was nine. He was then raised by his beloved stepmother, Sarah Lincoln, who encouraged him to read and study. Although Lincoln had a quick and inquiring mind, he suffered from bouts of depression throughout his life.

As a young man, Lincoln worked as a handyman, store clerk, militia volunteer, shopkeeper, postmaster, surveyor, and in any job that required a strong back. Elected to the Illinois General Assembly in 1834, Lincoln became a lawyer two years later. In 1846 he was elected from Illinois to the U.S. House of Representatives, but was defeated for the Senate in 1855 and 1858. He won the presidency in 1860 as a Republican.

By the time Abraham Lincoln was inaugurated on March 4, 1861, seven Southern states had seceded from the

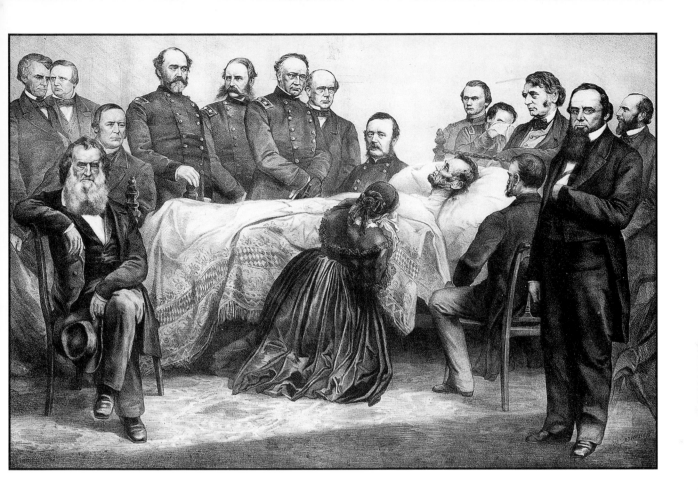

Union to form the Confederate States of America. On April 12, 1861, the war between the North and South began. The Civil War would decide the fate of slavery and states' rights. It would also decide if the Union could survive.

When Abraham Lincoln was sworn in for a second term on March 4, 1865, the end of the Civil War was in sight. Lincoln's main concern became how he could successfully bring the South back into the Union. He wouldn't live to carry out his plans.

As the long night wore on, Mrs. Lincoln came into the back bedroom from time to time, crying uncontrollably. By three in the morning, she was exhausted. She put her

A dying Abraham Lincoln was surrounded by grieving family, friends, government officials, and Army staff.

face close to Lincoln's. "Love, live but one moment to speak to our children," she pleaded. "Oh, oh that my little Taddy might see his father before he died."

At that moment, Lincoln gave a great rasping rattle. With a shriek, Mrs. Lincoln fell in a faint.

Secretary of War Stanton had earlier seized command of the situation. "Take that woman out and do not let her in again!" he ordered.

Mrs. Lincoln was escorted down the hall. "Oh, my God, and have I given my husband to die!" she cried. She would never see him again.

Rain began falling as a gray dawn lightened the Washington sky. President Lincoln's breathing became more labored and his pulse grew weaker. At 7:22 AM, April 15, 1865, Abraham Lincoln gave up the struggle. "It is all

Although the artist painted a black-garbed Mary Lincoln at her husband's East Room funeral service, she was not present.

over! The president is no more!" was the doctors' blunt announcement to Mary Lincoln.

The silence in the deathroom was broken only by Robert's weeping. Lincoln's minister then said a prayer and Secretary Stanton stepped forward to eulogize the slain president of the United States. "Now he belongs to the ages."

Shock reverberated across the country. Presidents William Henry Harrison and Zachary Taylor had both died in office of natural causes. But President Lincoln had been assassinated!

After an autopsy was performed in the White House, Lincoln's open coffin was placed on a catafalque in the East Room. On April 18 the line of citizens who came to pay their respects was so long that it took six hours to gain entrance. The following day six hundred invited guests attended the White House funeral. Neither Mary Lincoln, who was in a state of collapse, nor twelve-year-old Tad was present.

After the two-hour service, the hearse bearing Lincoln's coffin left the White House. Black troops led a three-mile-long procession to the Capitol. Although Tad rode with his brother Robert in a carriage directly behind the hearse, Mary Lincoln remained secluded in her bedroom.

Lincoln's body lay in state in the Capitol rotunda for two days as thousands filed past his open coffin. On April 21 Lincoln's coffin and Willie Lincoln's small coffin, which were placed on a special railroad car, began a 12-day journey to Springfield, Illinois, for burial. Along the way, the train stopped at eleven cities. At each stop, the president's coffin was taken off the train and carried in an elaborate procession to an appropriate resting place. The coffin was then opened for viewing by the public. As the train slowly moved westward, mourners lined the railroad tracks, kneeling, singing hymns, and lighting bonfires as the train passed.

On May 4, 1865, Abraham Lincoln and his son were buried in Springfield's Oak Ridge Cemetery. Out of a population of thirty-five million people, eight million Americans had participated in some way in a national outpouring of grief for the man who had led their country through its most perilous hour.

THE REBEL ACTOR

Twenty-six-year-old John Wilkes Booth was a handsome, vain young actor from a famous theatrical family. He was also a devoted supporter of slavery and the Confederacy. He wasn't, however, devoted enough to enlist in the Confederate Army; instead, he made plans to kidnap that "tyrant," Abraham Lincoln.

Mary Surratt's Washington boardinghouse became the headquarters for a motley crew of drifters that Booth gathered together. In the spring of 1865, Booth decided that kidnapping was too good for Lincoln. He deserved to die. Although several of the conspirators balked at murder and deserted, three others remained deeply involved: George Atzerodt, David Herold, and Lewis Powell.

On April 14, 1865, Booth learned that the Lincolns would be at Ford's Theatre that evening. Electrified at the prospect, Booth made plans with his co-conspirators.

Booth would assassinate the president. Atzerodt was to assassinate Vice-President Andrew Johnson in his hotel room. Powell and Herold would murder Secretary of State William Seward at his home. With those three men dead, the government would collapse in chaos.

Booth, who was well known at Ford's Theatre, gained entrance easily. During the day of April 14, he made careful preparations for the night ahead. About 10:15 P.M. that evening, he climbed to the upper lobby and opened the door that Parker had left unguarded. Barring the door behind him, he made his way down the hallway that led to the state box. Peering through a peephole that had earlier been bored in the state box door, he saw Lincoln seated right in front of him.

Booth quietly opened the door, shot the president, stabbed Major Rathbone, and leapt over the railing. But his spur caught in a flag that decorated the state box. When he landed on the stage, he broke the shinbone in his left leg. He hobbled out the back exit, mounted the horse he had waiting, and headed for the bridge leading to Maryland.

Meanwhile, George Atzerodt lost his nerve. Instead of killing Vice-President Johnson, he spent the evening in a nearby bar. Lewis Powell had no such misgivings. Led to Secretary of State Seward's home by David Herold, Powell viciously stabbed Seward and wounded members of Seward's household. Only a metal neck brace that Seward wore as the result of an earlier accident saved his life.

Although Powell was soon captured, Herold escaped to join Booth in Maryland. Booth, who was in agony from his

The poster reads:

War Department, Washington, April 20, 1865.

$100,000 REWARD!

THE MURDERER

Of our late beloved President, ABRAHAM LINCOLN,

IS STILL AT LARGE.

$50,000 REWARD!

will be paid by this Department for his apprehension, in addition to any reward offered by Municipal Authorities or State Executives.

$25,000 REWARD!

will be paid for the apprehension of JOHN H. SURRATT, one of Booth's accomplices.

$25,000 REWARD!

will be paid for the apprehension of DANIEL C. HARROLD, another of Booth's accomplices.

LIBERAL REWARDS will be paid for any information that shall conduce to the arrest of either of the above-named criminals, or their accomplices.

All persons harboring or secreting the said persons, or either of them, or aiding or assisting their concealment or escape, will be treated as accomplices in the murder of the President and the attempted assassination of the Secretary of State, and shall be subject to trial before a Military Commission and the punishment of DEATH.

Let the stain of innocent blood be removed from the land by the arrest and punishment of the murderers.

All good citizens are exhorted to aid public justice on this occasion. Every man should consider his own conscience charged with this solemn duty, and rest neither night nor day until it be accomplished.

EDWIN M. STANTON, Secretary of War.

DESCRIPTIONS.—BOOTH is 5 feet 7 or 8 inches high, slender build, high forehead, black hair, black eyes, and wears a heavy black moustache.

JOHN H. SURRATT is about 5 feet 9 inches. Hair rather thin and dark; eyes rather light; no beard. Would weigh 145 or 150 pounds. Complexion rather pale and clear, with color in his cheeks. Wore light clothes of fine quality. Shoulders square; cheek bones rather prominent; chin narrow; ears projecting at the top; forehead rather low and square, but broad. Parts his hair on the right side; neck rather long. His lips are firmly set. A slim man.

DANIEL C. HARROLD is 22 years of age, 5 feet 6 or 7 inches high, rather broad shouldered, otherwise light built; dark hair, little (if any) moustache; dark eyes; weighs about 140 pounds.

GEO. F. NESBITT & CO., Printers and Stationers, cor. Pearl and Pine Streets, N. Y.

broken leg, penned an entry in his diary: "Our country owed all her troubles to him [Lincoln], and God simply made me the instrument of his punishment."

After eight days in hiding, Booth and Herold fled from Maryland into Virginia. But Union troops tracked them down. At 2 A.M. on April 26, soldiers surrounded the tobacco barn where the two men were sleeping. Although Herold gave himself up, Booth refused to surrender. An officer set fire to the barn. A shot was fired. Booth fell, fatally wounded. It was never known if Booth was shot by a soldier's bullet or his own.

That morning, as Booth lay dying in excruciating pain, he murmured, "Tell Mother I die for my country." Booth's body was returned to Washington on the *Montauk*, the same ship that Lincoln had toured on the day he was shot.

Lewis Powell, David Herold, George Atzerodt, and Mary Surratt were arrested, as were the three men who had rejected Booth's assassination plot, and a Maryland doctor who had set Booth's leg. Because Lincoln had been commander-in-chief of the armed forces, Secretary of war Edwin Stanton ordered a military trial.

Powell, Herold, Atzerodt, and Surratt received the death penalty. The other four men were sentenced to life imprisonment. One man died in prison while the other three were later pardoned. With doubts raised about Surratt's

When John Wilkes Booth refused to surrender, federal troops set fire to the barn where he was hiding.

role, there was a public outcry against her death sentence. It was to no avail. The four conspirators were hanged on July 7, 1865.

THE GRIM PRESIDENT

A stunned Vice-President Andrew Johnson took the presidential oath of office at 10 A.M., April 15, 1865, in a Washington hotel room. Johnson, who was a Democrat from Tennessee, had been the only Southern senator to remain loyal to the Union. As president, he now found himself responsible for dealing with the thorny problems of the South's Reconstruction.

Andrew Johnson tried to follow Abraham Lincoln's policy of warmly welcoming the South back into the family of the United States. But Radical Republicans in Congress saw an opportunity to grab power after Lincoln's death and opposed Johnson on every issue. They had no intention of treating the South with charity. They wanted to punish the South as a defeated enemy nation, as well as to restrict the Southern white vote, which was traditionally Democratic. Assuming that freed slaves would support Republican candidates, Radical Republicans also wanted former slaves to be granted the vote.

When Johnson became president in April, Congress had already left Washington for its eight-month recess. With Congress gone, Johnson pardoned high-ranking Confederate leaders. And every Southern state that had seceded from the Union, except Texas, was allowed to elect representatives and senators to Congress.

When the Senate and the House of Representatives reconvened in December, the Radical Republicans were furious at what Johnson had done. They first delayed the seating of the new Southern members of Congress. By a two-thirds vote, they then passed two civil rights bills that President Johnson had earlier vetoed. Again and again, Radical Republicans in Congress passed bills by a two-thirds majority vote over Johnson's vetoes.

Frustrated and angry, Johnson decided to take his case to the country. He had always been dedicated to the needs of the working people, and, as a man without schooling, had driven himself to study all his life. He was also a staunch supporter of the Union and the Constitution.

But Andrew Johnson was no Abraham Lincoln. On his speaking tour, he lost his temper and argued with anyone who disagreed with him. He allowed hecklers to draw him into ugly shouting matches. Angry and quarrelsome, Johnson gained little public support.

As a result, Republicans won an even greater majority in the 1866 congressional elections. By overriding President Johnson's vetoes, Congress dictated military rule and harsh controls on the South. Congress also passed an act called the Tenure of Office Act, which barred the president from firing any official whose appointment had needed Senate approval. Declaring the act unconstitutional, Johnson fired his Radical Republican secretary of war, Edwin Stanton.

On March 6, 1868, the Sergeant-at-Arms of the Senate served President Andrew Johnson with a summons to appear before the Senate.

With that, the House of Representatives voted to impeach Johnson for "high crimes and misdemeanors." A two-thirds majority of the Senate was needed to remove the president from office.

After a two-and-a-half-month trial in the spring of 1868, Johnson's presidency was saved by a single Senate vote and he finished out the rest of his term. But the Democratic party refused to nominate him for president in 1868 despite his achievements: acquiring the Midway Islands, buying Alaska from the Russians, and pardoning all Southerners who had taken part in the Civil War.

In 1875 Andrew Johnson returned to Washington as the Democratic senator from Tennessee. Only three months later, on July 31, 1875, he suffered a stroke and died.

DASHED HOPES

Abraham Lincoln led the nation through four terrible years of war. His next challenge was to bring healing to both the North and the South. Despite Radical Republican opposition in Congress, he was determined to treat the South with compassion.

If anyone could have won the peace, it would have been Lincoln. Not only was Lincoln a master politician, but he also had enormous prestige as the commander in chief of the victorious Northern army. He was able to promise freedom and citizenship to former slaves and forgiveness to Southern whites. He also promised security to the North, which needed reassurance that the South would never mount another rebellion.

After Lincoln's death, President Andrew Johnson tried to follow Lincoln's policies. But he was stubborn and hot-tempered, ignored public opinion, and didn't know how to gain support for his programs. Johnson's efforts to bring the South back into the United States harmoniously were a failure. Booth's bullet did more than kill a great president. It also dashed any hope of a just and reasonable peace.

JULY 2, 1881

At seven o'clock on a hot July morning, the president's fifteen-year-old son, Jim, came into his father's White House bedroom. They chatted a few minutes and then joined seventeen-year-old Hal in his room. For a while the president and his sons lay in bed and talked about the duties of the presidency.

All of a sudden, the president's mood changed and he started singing "I Mixed Those Children Up." It was his favorite tune from the new operetta H.M.S. Pinafore. That got the three of them going and they began to roughhouse. Jim did a handspring over the bed and challenged his father to do one, too. Although the president's beard and thinning hair made him look older than forty-nine, he was muscular and athletic. Besides, he couldn't resist a challenge. He turned a handspring over the bed as easily as Jim had.

The president and his boys were feeling frisky for good reason. In just a few hours they would be taking a train to meet the rest of the family to start their summer vacation.

The president dressed in a new gray suit, placed a flower in his buttonhole, and went downstairs. His secretary of state was waiting for him. As soon as the two men had breakfast, they climbed into the secretary's carriage for the drive to the railroad station.

THE SUMMER OF THE PRESIDENT

JAMES ABRAM GARFIELD
November 19, 1831–September 19, 1881
Twentieth President, 1881

THE BALTIMORE & POTOMAC RAILROAD DEPOT

President James A. Garfield and his secretary of state, James Blaine, pulled up to the Baltimore & Potomac Railroad Depot at 9:30 A.M. on July 2, 1881. The president's aide, Colonel Almon Rockwell, was following in another carriage with young Hal and Jim Garfield.

The president and Blaine entered the Ladies' Waiting Room. As they headed toward the main waiting room, a man approached the president from behind. He pulled a pistol out of his pocket. There was a sudden explosion. The president flung his arms up in the air.

"My God," he cried. "What is this?"

Another shot rang out. The president's legs buckled and he fell to the floor.

The woman in charge of the Ladies' Waiting Room screamed as the man with the pistol fled. Blaine's immediate reaction was to give chase. But when he realized that the president had been hit, he quickly turned back.

Police officer Patrick Kearney was on duty at the exit. Hearing the shots, he ran inside, only to bump into a man

President Garfield was shot in the back by an assassin's bullet.

racing for the door. Though Officer Kearney didn't know what had happened, he grabbed the man. Charles J. Guiteau didn't resist. He had shot the president. He knew he would be arrested and welcomed the chance to be heard.

Hal, Jim, and Colonel Rockwell were outside checking their luggage when they, too, heard the shots. Alarmed, they ran into the depot. To their horror, they found President Garfield lying on the floor, his new suit covered with blood. He was conscious but in shock. One bullet had grazed his arm. The other had entered his back just above his waist. He whispered a few words to his frightened son Hal and then vomited.

The depot was in an uproar as word of the shooting spread. Three cabinet officers who had been waiting for the president on the train platform hurried to his side. Frantic calls went out for a doctor. A mattress was found in a sleeping car and Garfield was laid on it. As Kearney and another officer hustled Guiteau out of the depot, bystanders yelled: "Lynch him! Hang the murderer!"

The city health officer was the first doctor to arrive. He quickly examined Garfield and probed the wound with his finger in an unsuccessful attempt to find the bullet. When Garfield asked for his opinion, the doctor tried to sound optimistic.

Shaking his head, Garfield murmured, "I thank you, Doctor, but I am a dead man."

With more and more people crowding into the Ladies' Waiting Room, the president was carried on the mattress to an empty second-floor room. Hal and Jim followed their father up the stairs. Jim wept as Hal tried to comfort him.

Dr. Willard Bliss, a prominent Washington physician, was rushed to the depot by carriage. Other doctors heard of the shooting and hurried to the scene, too.

Although it was known that germs could cause infection and disease, most doctors of the time didn't put much faith in the theory. Dr. Bliss pushed an unsterile Nélaton probe into the wound to try and locate the bullet. A Nélaton probe was a long thin instrument with a white porcelain head. If the porcelain head came in contact with a lead bullet, the lead left a distinct mark on the porcelain. At least three other doctors probed the wound with their fingers.

Garfield, who was still conscious, worried that his wife would learn of the shooting from reporters. He asked Colonel Rockwell to telegraph her. "Tell her I am seriously hurt," he ordered. "How seriously I cannot yet say. I am myself and hope she will come to me soon. I send my love to her."

Lucretia Garfield was recovering from malaria at the New Jersey seashore. With her was the Garfields' fourteen-year-old daughter, Mollie. The Garfield family was to have been reunited later that day to begin their vacation. Only the two youngest boys, who were on their way by train to visit Garfield relatives in Ohio, wouldn't be joining them.

James Abram Garfield and Lucretia Rudolph had both been seventeen-year-old students in rural Ohio when they first met. Always known as Crete, Lucretia was shy and bookish. After an on-again, off-again courtship, they were married on November 11, 1858, in Hiram, Ohio. Their marriage had a shaky beginning, but as the years passed, they came to realize how much they loved each other. They had five children: Harry Abram, James Rudolph, Mary, Irvin McDowell, and Abram. Two other children died in infancy.

Now Garfield insisted on returning to the White House and his own bedroom. Eight men carried him to a waiting ambulance. The police surrounded the horse-drawn ambulance and lifted the wheels over the potholes to ease the president's journey. A horrified crowd silently followed the sad little procession.

Despite his pain, Garfield did his best to reassure Jim, who never left his side. "The upper story was not hurt. It was the hull," he said in an attempt at humor.

As Garfield was taken up to his bedroom, he saw Mrs. Blaine. He blew her a kiss. "Don't leave me until Crete comes," he pleaded. "Whatever happens, I want you to promise to look out for Crete."

Mrs. Garfield arrived from New Jersey early that evening with Mollie. Secretary of State Blaine wept to see Jim and his mother cling to one another. Although those who knew Lucretia Garfield expected her to collapse, she surprised everyone. Mrs. Blaine later described the First Lady as "frail, fatigued, desperate, but firm and quiet and full of purpose to save."

Garfield had been waiting anxiously for his beloved Crete. As soon as they were alone, he began to advise her what to do when he died. She interrupted him. "You are not going to die," she insisted. "I am here to nurse you back to life."

After some fifteen minutes, Garfield, who was a deeply religious man, urged her to get some rest. "I shall want you near me when the crisis comes," he said.

Even though the doctors were certain that Garfield would die that night, they continued to probe his wound with their fingers and unclean instruments. Why they did this is a mystery. Even if they had found the bullet, they wouldn't have dared operate. The doctors also tried to keep up Garfield's spirits. But Garfield was realistic as well as religious. "I am willing to lay down the heavy burden thrust upon me," he told them.

Meanwhile, Washington was close to rioting. Mobs threatened to storm the jail where Guiteau was being held. Secretary of War Robert Lincoln, Abraham Lincoln's son,

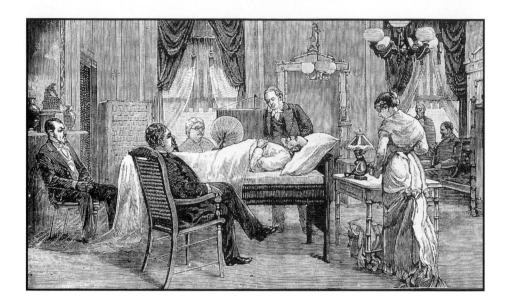

Mrs. Garfield (standing) and President Garfield's doctors were in constant attendance.

ordered troops to guard the jail and surround the White House. "My God, how many hours of sorrow I have passed in this town," Robert had exclaimed when he heard that another president had been cut down.

Only two nights before, Garfield had asked Robert Lincoln to tell him about his father's assassination. Robert had talked for more than an hour, reliving that terrible time.

Abraham Lincoln's death in 1865 had forced every succeeding president to face the possibility of assassination. Even so, Garfield never took seriously the threatening letters he received. Increased security by Washington's Metropolitan Police had been suggested, but Garfield wouldn't consider having police stationed at the White House. Earlier he had said: "Assassination can no more be guarded against than death by lightning; and it is best not to worry about either."

Incredibly, the day after the shooting, Garfield was better. July 3 was a Sunday and Americans flocked to churches to pray for their president. For the time being, old political battles were put aside. But those battles had been bitter.

James Garfield had been an Ohio delegate at the 1880 Republican convention to choose the party's candidate for president. At the convention, the Stalwart Republicans and the moderate Half-Breed Republicans argued angrily. The Stalwart Republicans wanted all government, or civil service, jobs to be appointed by politicians just as they had been for sixty years. Under this system, civil service jobs were used to reward those who supported the political party in power. Many of the people hired were unfit for their jobs. Even worse, a lot of them were dishonest. Garfield, who was a moderate Republican, wanted to reform the system.

To break the convention deadlock between the Stalwarts and the Half-Breeds, James Garfield was nominated on the thirty-sixth ballot to be the Republican candidate for the presidency. To keep the Stalwarts happy, Stalwart Chester A. Arthur became Garfield's vice-presidential running mate. The Garfield-Arthur ticket won the election in November 1880 by a pencil-thin majority.

Just before he was inaugurated on March 4, 1881, Garfield returned to Ohio for a funeral. "Today is a sort of burial day in many ways," he said. Although he was referring to the responsibility and isolation of the presidency, his comment was nearer to the truth than he could have guessed. Four months later, he was shot.

To everyone's amazement, Garfield survived the first three weeks and even seemed to be improving. But on July 23, he woke up with chills, a high fever, tremors, and vomiting. The probing of the wound with fingers and unsterile instruments had caused infection. Pus had formed in the channel that the doctors had created with their probes. The doctors operated and cleaned out the wound. They also removed a piece of bone from one of his broken ribs. Although Garfield was fully conscious, he didn't complain or cry out. "Never had physician such a patient before," Dr. Bliss remarked.

But the surgery took its toll, and Garfield went from crisis to crisis. Crete Garfield was with her husband constantly. She fixed him special food and fanned him. She held his hand and let him talk about the farm they had bought in Ohio.

In August, Garfield was operated on two more times to clean out the pus and infection. He was in constant pain. He couldn't sleep or hold down food. His weight dropped from 210 pounds to 130. Through it all, he remained polite and considerate. He even joked from time to time, although he was seen to smile only once.

Garfield's critical condition presented a problem. Article II of the Constitution didn't provide any means for deciding whether or not a president was able to fulfill the "Powers and Duties" of the presidency. Secretary of State Blaine suggested that Vice-President Arthur become acting president. Arthur wouldn't hear of it. Luckily for the country, Congress wasn't in session and the government had pretty much shut down for the summer.

Anyone who could get out of Washington had already left. But Garfield was trapped in the White House. The heat, humidity, and stench from the nearby Potomac River swamps were suffocating. To give the president some relief, Navy engineers rigged up a primitive air conditioning system.

Alexander Graham Bell, who had invented an electrical device similar to a modern mine detector, was summoned to try and locate the bullet. But the device, which was connected to a telephone receiver, failed to find the bullet.

"People must be tired of hearing of my symptoms," Garfield commented as the weeks dragged on.

He was mistaken. The summer of 1881 became the summer of the president. Every day crowds waited for news outside the White House gates. Newspapers published daily progress reports. Train stations posted medical updates. Special days of prayer were held.

Following in a long line of log-cabin presidents, Garfield held a special place in the hearts of the American people. Now his image as a folk hero soared to new heights. James Abram Garfield, who had been born in a log cabin in 1831, was one of four children raised by a wid-

Alexander Graham Bell (far right) failed to find the bullet with his metal detecting device.

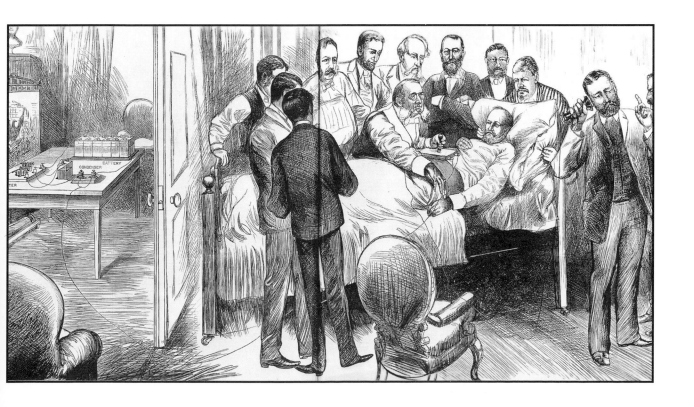

Reports on President Garfield's condition were posted daily.

owed mother in the Ohio wilderness. Young James worked at all sorts of jobs, mostly on neighboring farms. He even drove a mule on the Ohio and Erie Canal. Despite being large for his age, James was sickly, and he suffered periods of depression all his life.

After attending Western Reserve Eclectic Institute for two years, James graduated from Williams College in 1856. As an intellectual and a scholar, James preached, taught school, debated, became principal of Eclectic Institute, practiced law, and was elected to the Ohio Senate in 1859.

He fought with the Union Army during the Civil War, rising to the rank of major general. From 1863 to 1880, Garfield represented Ohio in the U.S. House of Representatives. In 1880 he was elected the twentieth president of the United States.

Folk hero or not, Garfield was only human. After two months of being poked, probed, and operated on, he was at the end of his patience. He demanded to leave Washington. The doctors finally agreed to let him travel to Elberon on the New Jersey seashore.

With Hal and Jim both students at Williams College, and Abe and Irvin still in Ohio, only Mrs. Garfield and Mollie accompanied the president. On September 6 they returned in an ambulance to the scene of the shooting, the Baltimore & Potomac Railroad Depot. A hospital bed had been set up in Garfield's private railroad car and right of way had been cleared for a non-stop trip. In Elberon volunteers had laid railroad tracks right up to the cottage door.

"I have always felt that the ocean was my friend and the sight of it brings rest and peace," Garfield had once remarked. When he was propped up where he could see, hear, and smell the ocean, his spirits rose. "This is delightful, it is such a change," he said.

Only nine days later, his old foes returned: fever, chills, an irregular pulse, and vomiting. He was suffering from infection, blood poisoning, and pneumonia. He knew that this time he wouldn't make it.

"My work is done," he said.

"O why am I made to suffer this cruel wrong!" Mrs. Garfield cried when she was told that the end was near.

James Abram Garfield died at 10:35 P.M. on September 19, 1881, with his wife and daughter at his side. "It is over," Dr. Bliss said quietly.

The doctors performed an autopsy the next day. "We made a mistake," one of them admitted when they found the bullet. They certainly had. Although the bullet had entered to the right of Garfield's spine, it had traveled downward and to the left. For months, the doctors had been probing for the bullet on Garfield's right side. Alexander Graham Bell hadn't been able to find the bullet because he had followed the doctors' directions and placed his device in the wrong position.

A cyst had formed around the bullet, rendering it harmless. With proper medical care, Garfield could have been up and back to work in a few weeks. Instead, the constant probing and operations, which were performed under unsterile conditions, introduced more bacteria and infection into his body. And lying in bed for months had only made him weaker and sicker.

The same train that had taken Garfield to Elberon returned his body to Washington. Thousands of citizens lined the route. Their hats were off and they wept as their president's black-draped railroad car passed. For many, it must have brought back memories of Lincoln's funeral train sixteen years before.

Of the eight presidents who have died in office, Garfield was the only one whose body didn't lie in state in the White House East Room. Instead, his body was taken directly to the Capitol rotunda. Perhaps that was because his political life had been spent in the House of

Representatives. More than likely, it was because the State Rooms of the White House were being painted and remodeled, and the East Room was in disrepair.

Although Garfield was president for less than two hundred days, it didn't matter to the American people. This was their elected president who had been felled by an assassin's bullet. For two days, more than seventy thousand mourners lined up at the Capitol rotunda to pay their respects. On September 26, 1881, President Garfield was buried in Cleveland, Ohio, close by the waters of Lake Erie that he loved.

THE JOB SEEKER

The public never forgot that Abraham Lincoln had been killed by a conspiracy headed by John Wilkes Booth. The nation now assumed that a conspiracy had plotted President Garfield's death, too. But Charles Julius Guiteau had acted alone.

Guiteau had been a failure all his adult life. He was a fraud, cheat, and chronic liar. He was always on the run from bad debts. He had served time in jail.

Guiteau had been obsessed with religion for years. He even wrote a book about the Bible, which he paid to have printed. In 1880 Guiteau turned from religion to politics. Two days after Garfield became president, Guiteau showed up at the White House. He returned almost every day, leaving letters and notes and demanding to see the president. Guiteau was convinced that he should be appointed as the chief American diplomat in either Vienna or Paris.

Guiteau was only one of thousands of job seekers who lined up at the White House to see the president. Although Garfield had earlier talked of reforming the civil service system, once he was in office, he didn't try to stop the greedy scramble for government jobs. He was soon overwhelmed. "These people would take my very brain, flesh and blood, if they could," he complained.

Guiteau became more and more of a nuisance to Garfield's staff. On May 13, 1881, he was banned from the White House altogether. Five days later, he had what he called an inspiration. It was the will of God that he should "remove" the president. Certain that he would be hailed as a hero, he bought a large pearl-handled revolver that would look impressive when displayed in a museum.

Guiteau stalked the president. He sat for hours across from the White House, watching Garfield come and go. He came close to shooting the president several times, but conditions weren't to his liking. Before the day that he shot Garfield, Guiteau penned a letter to the White House. "The president's tragic death was a sad necessity, but it will unite the Republican party and save the Republic," he wrote. "I had no ill-will to the president. His death was a political necessity."

"He must be insane," the president later commented from his White House bedroom. "None but an insane person could have done such a thing."

Two months after the president's death, Guiteau went on trial. Garfield had been right. Guiteau was insane. Several people close to Guiteau testified to that fact. So did a doctor who had examined Guiteau after he had threatened to kill his own sister. Although Guiteau's brother-in-law, who was his lawyer, pleaded insanity, the law stated that a defendant was considered sane if he knew what he was doing at the time of his crime.

During the trial, Guiteau laughed, told stories, acted as his own lawyer, and insulted the judge, lawyers, and witnesses. Testifying with lies, jokes, and boasting, he never accepted responsibility for killing President Garfield.

Public anger ran high and Guiteau was the target of

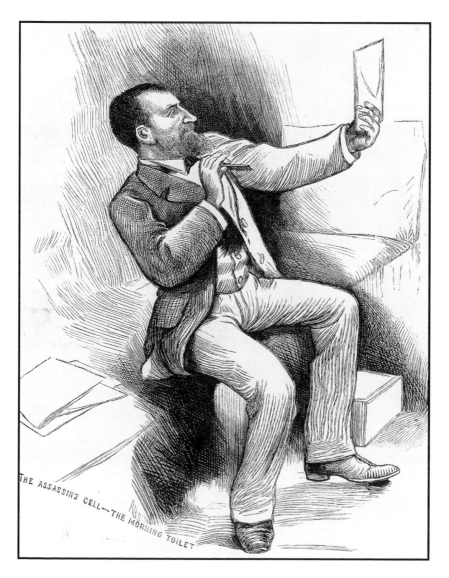

THE ASSASSIN'S CELL—THE MORNING TOILET

Charles Guiteau primped in his cell before his court appearance.

three shootings, twice when he was in jail and once as he rode to court in the prison van. None of the attempts was successful.

On January 25, 1882, the bizarre two-and-a-half-month trial was over. After deliberating for only sixty-five minutes, the jury declared Charles Julius Guiteau guilty. He was hanged on June 30, 1882.

THE STALWART PRESIDENT

When police officers led Charles Guiteau from the railroad depot he announced: "I did it, and will go to jail for it. Arthur is president and I am a Stalwart." Americans' first reaction was that Vice-President Chester Alan Arthur might have had something to do with President Garfield's assassination. After all, Arthur was a Stalwart Republican.

Arthur's reputation was already questionable. For seven years he had been the highly paid Collector of the Port of New York, which employed more than a thousand people. He used his office to reward Republican party workers with jobs. In 1878 President Rutherford B. Hayes had fired him. The country might not have tolerated Arthur as its president if Garfield had died at the time he was shot.

Over the long summer of Garfield's dying, however, Arthur handled himself with grace and dignity. He stayed home in seclusion. He refused to become acting president. He made proper courtesy calls on Mrs. Garfield. By the time he became president, he had earned the respect of the American people. Chester Arthur was sworn in as

Chester Arthur took the oath of office in his New York home, September 20, 1881.

president at 2:15 A.M. on September 20, 1881, in his New York City townhouse.

Because Arthur was faced with a horrified and grieving nation, he was eager to gain the American people's confidence and prove himself worthy to be president. With his reputation for shady political practices, he knew that he had to deal quickly with any kind of scandal.

Arthur immediately ordered that illegal practices in the Post Office Department be prosecuted "with the utmost vigor of the law." He even appointed two Democrats to handle most of the investigation. Knowing that Americans believed Guiteau was a disappointed job seeker, he pressed Congress to reform the civil service system.

In 1883 Arthur signed the Pendleton Act into law. Written examinations open to all citizens would be required for certain government jobs. New employees would be selected on the basis of their grades. No one could be fired for political reasons. The law also created the Civil Service Commission, which supervised, and still supervises, the selection of government workers. Thanks to Arthur's efforts, the new law was as much of a memorial to Garfield as the towering stone monument that was erected over his Ohio grave.

But Arthur was unsuccessful at ending the feud between Stalwart and Half-Breed Republicans. Without solid Republican support, he was unable to win his party's nomination for president in 1884. Chester Arthur died in New York City on November 18, 1886, only a year and a half after leaving office.

ONLY TWO HUNDRED DAYS

During his first months in office, James Garfield had hesitated to make changes in the civil service system. He had won the presidency by such a narrow margin, perhaps he was reluctant to take action. Or it may be that he had future plans to reform the system. It wasn't as if Garfield lacked courage. Early in his administration he'd had the courage to appoint Half-Breed Republicans to important positions against powerful Stalwart opposition.

What Garfield might have accomplished will never be known. He was president for less than two hundred days and for much of that time, he was a helpless invalid.

Garfield's life, like Lincoln's, had begun in a wilderness log cabin and been ended by an assassin's bullet. Abraham Lincoln, however, had served a full term as wartime president. The Civil War was the nation's bloodiest war and Lincoln's assassination had been the ultimate horror after four years of horror.

Unlike Lincoln's assassination, Garfield's assassination had followed sixteen years of peace. His death made frighteningly clear to the American people that their president could be cut down at any time, in any place, for any reason.

SEPTEMBER 6, 1901

The president and First Lady were looking forward to a "restful day" at Niagara Falls with friends. Although the early September weather was hot and humid, the president wore his usual frock coat, vest, pin striped trousers, stiff white shirt, black satin necktie, gloves, and top hat.

The president, his wife, and their guests left Buffalo by train for the short ride to Niagara Falls. They first took a trolley that ran along the Niagara gorge and rapids. The president's party next boarded carriages to view spectacular Horseshoe Falls with its thundering roar, boiling waters, and magnificent rainbow.

But the First Lady wasn't well and the excitement and heat were too much for her. Thoughtful and considerate of his wife as always, the president escorted her to a nearby hotel to rest. He then rejoined his companions for more sightseeing.

After lunch, the president, First Lady, and their guests headed back to Buffalo on the train. Knowing that his "restful day" was over, the president asked his manservant for a clean collar. He wanted to freshen up for his appearance at a four o'clock reception. Although his staff worried that he was exposing himself to danger, the president had agreed to shake hands with anyone who wanted to meet him.

"NEARER MY GOD TO THEE"

WILLIAM McKINLEY

January 29, 1843–September 14, 1901
Twenty-fifth President, 1897–1901

THE TEMPLE OF MUSIC

President and Mrs. William McKinley arrived in Buffalo, New York, on September 4, 1901. They were to spend two days at the Pan-American Exposition, which had been organized to further understanding between North and South America. On September 5 the president gave a speech on the Exposition grounds to nearly fifty thousand people. After a tour of Niagara Falls on the morning of September 6, the president was scheduled to greet the public at four o'clock in the Temple of Music.

Although Mrs. McKinley had planned to attend the reception with her husband, she was exhausted from her trip to Niagara Falls. She would go for a carriage ride instead, and then rest.

The president bid her farewell. "Good afternoon, Mrs. McKinley," he said. "I hope you will enjoy your ride; good-bye." He raised his top hat and waved.

It was almost four o'clock by the time McKinley arrived at the Temple of Music. As the president's carriage came into view, the waiting crowd cheered and applauded. McKinley was short and stout, but his appearance was dig-

President and Mrs. McKinley drew huge crowds at the Pan-American Exposition.

nified and impressive. Hearing the enthusiastic welcome, the organist inside the hall played "The Star-Spangled Banner." The people opened a path for McKinley to enter.

Major Louis Babcock, who was in charge of arrangements, had asked John Milburn, president of the Exposition, and George Cortelyou, McKinley's secretary, to join the president in the receiving line. As a security precaution, potted palms, bay trees, and American flags had been placed behind the three men so that no one could approch the president from the rear.

McKinley nodded at Babcock to open the door. "Let them come," he directed.

The people entered the Temple of Music two by two. As

they approached the president to shake his hand, they narrowed to a single line. This was President McKinley at his best. Despite his rather stiff manner and formal dress, he was a genuinely warm person.

At seven minutes past four, the organ was playing a Bach sonata when a small, neatly dressed man in a plain gray suit and workman's cap stepped up to the president. Noticing that the man's right hand was bandaged in a handkerchief, McKinley reached out to shake his left hand. But the man shoved the president's hand aside and sprang forward. Two shots cracked out. Smoke rose from the handkerchief. For a suspended moment the two men were locked face-to-face. Shivering, McKinley straightened up to his full height and then staggered backward.

A detective was the first to reach the president. As oth-

Despite stepped-up security, a gunman shot President McKinley at point-blank range.

ers rushed to McKinley's side and helped him into a chair, guards threw the gunman to the floor. After seizing his pistol, they battered him with blows and punches.

McKinley saw that his attacker was being savagely beaten. "Don't let them hurt him," he murmured.

The sudden noise and confusion shattered the stunned silence. Panicked, the people stampeded toward the doors. For the third time in thirty-six years, a president had been shot down in a public place in the presence of horrified witnesses.

As the men closest to McKinley fanned him with their hats, he fingered his chest and stomach. When he put his hand on his secretary's shoulder, it was covered with blood. "My wife," he whispered, "be careful, Cortelyou, how you tell her—oh, be careful."

By this time guards had surrounded the bloody and half-conscious gunman. The policemen on duty outside shouldered their way in and cleared everyone from the hall. A little electric ambulance came clanging up. Attendants jumped out. The people who had opened a path for McKinley to enter the Temple of Music minutes before, now opened a path for him to be carried out on a stretcher.

A loud moan went up at the sight of the president's ashen face and blood-soaked clothes. The onlookers were so enraged that when the gunman emerged in police custody, they could hardly be restrained from mobbing and killing him. The police had already learned his name— Leon F. Czolgosz. He called himself an anarchist.

Anarchists believe that the only good government is no

An electric ambulance rushed President McKinley to the Exposition's makeshift hospital.

government. Although not all anarchists of McKinley's time favored violence, some did. One anarchist group had drawn up a list of world leaders whom they planned to assassinate. The list, which was in Secret Service files, included President McKinley's name and was no idle threat. Since 1894 anarchists had assassinated the president of France, the empress of Austria, and the king of Italy. Five months earlier, Great Britain's Prince of Wales had narrowly escaped an anarchist's bullet.

The Secret Service, which the Treasury Department had

Secret Serviceman George Foster (in derby) stayed close to McKinley (in top hat) on the trip to Niagara Falls.

originally organized to catch counterfeiters, had recently expanded its authority to protect the president. In response to threats, a full-time Secret Serviceman, George Foster, was assigned to McKinley. In theory, Foster went where the president went. But McKinley didn't like to be closely guarded and he often slipped away. He also didn't want to give the impression that he was isolated from the people.

President McKinley had been repeatedly warned that making a public appearance at the Temple of Music was risky. Cortelyou, his secretary, had taken the reception off the president's schedule twice and twice McKinley had put it back on. On their way to Buffalo, Cortelyou had again urged McKinley to cancel the reception.

"Why should I?" McKinley had asked. "No one would wish to hurt me."

All Cortelyou could do was request more protection.

Major Babcock had already assigned guards to the Temple of Music. But on the day of the reception, an acquaintance casually remarked to Babcock that it would just be young, aggressive Vice-President Theodore Roosevelt's luck to have someone shoot the president. Babcock was so alarmed at the thought that he tightened security.

He stationed twelve Exposition police outside the Temple of Music. Inside, the public would have to pass through two lines of policemen and soldiers. Five Buffalo detectives and three Secret Servicemen were posted near the president, with two soldiers on either side of the receiving line.

Although the president appeared to be well protected, he wasn't. Secret Serviceman George Foster should have been stationed behind the president and to his left. Instead, Foster and Secret Serviceman Samuel Ireland were posted three feet away, facing the president. The third Secret Serviceman stood ten feet to McKinley's right. None of them had a clear view of the approaching line, nor were they in a position to defend the president in case of trouble.

Standard procedure was that every person greeting the president should have hands that were visible and empty. Yet the man whose right hand was wrapped in a bulging handkerchief was never questioned. When Czolgosz fired his gun, Secret Serviceman Ireland's hand was actually on Czolgosz's shoulder to move the line along more quickly.

Ten minutes after the shooting, McKinley was in the Exposition hospital. Although it wasn't much more than a first aid station, he was taken to the little operating room.

He was in shock, but conscious and calm. One bullet, which had grazed his ribs, fell out of his clothes. The other bullet had torn into his abdomen.

Eleven doctors responded to the call that the president had been shot. But it wasn't until a well-known society surgeon arrived that the doctors prepared to operate. Always a religious man, McKinley repeated the Lord's Prayer as he went under ether.

The lighting in the operating room was poor. Dr. Presley Rixey, McKinley's White House physician, held up a hand mirror to reflect the rays of the sun on the surgeons' field of work.

The doctors couldn't find the bullet that had gone through McKinley's stomach walls, and their patient was too weak for them to probe for it. Instead, the surgeon cleaned out the wound and repaired the ragged tears. The only doctor present who was an expert on gunshot wounds advised placing a drain in the wound to remove fluids, blood, and infectious materials. But the other doctors rejected his advice, and the surgeon closed the wound without a drain.

After the hour-and-a-half operation, the president was taken to John Milburn's house where he and the First Lady were staying. Dr. Rixey hurried on ahead. He knew how high-strung and nervous Mrs. McKinley was, and he wanted to be the one to break the news.

William McKinley had been a twenty-six-year-old prosecuting attorney in Canton, Ohio, when he and Ida Saxton met and fell in love. Ida was a frail, attractive, rather spoiled young woman from a prominent Canton family. Married on January 25, 1871, William and Ida had their first child, Katherine, the following December. In 1873 Ida's mother died. Shortly after her death the McKinleys had a second daughter, Ida, who lived only five months. Three years later their daughter Katherine died.

Ida McKinley never recovered from these tragedies, either emotionally or physically. She became a lifelong, self-centered invalid who was totally dependent on her husband. She suffered from depression, headaches, spells of hysteria, and epileptic seizures. McKinley always sat or stood next to his wife at social affairs. At the first sign of a seizure, he would place a napkin or handkerchief over her face and lead her from the room. Despite his wife's constant demands, he never complained, and the McKinleys seemed devoted to each other.

When the president was carried into the Milburn house, he was unconscious and moaning. Everyone assumed that Mrs. McKinley would collapse in hysterics. On the contrary, she remained calm. All she asked was that her husband be brought to her room. But the doctors and nurses settled him in a separate bedroom.

Dismay and horror swept the nation. Only a brief account of the shooting made the Friday evening newspapers. That night people flocked to newspaper bulletin boards for news. Cortelyou's first statement reported that doctors had operated. His second statement, which announced that the president was resting comfortably, was met by a national sigh of relief.

As the weekend passed, the attempted assassination was all anyone talked about. Comparisons were made with

President Garfield's assassination twenty years before. Both men were struck at close range by two bullets, one harmless and the other causing a critical wound.

There were more similarities between the two Republican presidents than their injuries. They were both natives of frontier Ohio. The seventh of nine children, William McKinley was born on January 29, 1843, in Niles, Ohio. As a child, McKinley, like Garfield, was a good student, but sickly. Although he entered Allegheny College at seventeen, illness forced him to leave after one term. Lacking the money to return, he never finished. Instead, he became a schoolteacher and worked in a post office.

Both Garfield and McKinley enlisted in the Union army during the Civil War. Serving in some of the war's bloodiest battles, McKinley rose to the rank of major. His commanding officer, Rutherford B. Hayes, later President Hayes, described McKinley as "one of the bravest and finest officers in the army."

McKinley, who became a lawyer after the war, was elected county prosecutor in Canton, Ohio, in 1869. Like Garfield, Republican McKinley represented Ohio in the House of Representatives. He served in the House from 1877 to 1883 and 1885 to 1891. In 1891 he was elected governor of Ohio. When he ran for president in 1896, his friend and advisor, millionaire businessman Mark Hanna, raised most of the money needed for his campaign. William McKinley won the election and was inaugurated twenty-fifth president of the United States on March 4, 1897.

Now, six months into McKinley's second term, the eyes of the world were focused on Buffalo. John Milburn's handsome brick house became a hospital. The stables were turned into offices. Tents were set up for the press. The street was roped off and patrolled by soldiers.

McKinley's Ohio relatives traveled to Buffalo by special train. Vice-President Theodore Roosevelt and other government leaders arrived the day after the shooting. Robert Lincoln, who had witnessed so much tragedy, came to Buffalo to pay his respects.

On Monday McKinley was better. On Tuesday he was even stronger. With the doctors' reassurance that the president would recover, Vice-President Roosevelt and other government officials left Buffalo. The doctors even turned down Thomas Edison's offer to use a new medical invention, an X-ray machine.

Secretary of State John Hay arrived as everyone else was leaving. Unlike the others, he was pessimistic about McKinley's recovery. Maybe that was because this was the third president he had served under who had been shot. Hay had been Lincoln's private secretary, Garfield's assistant secretary of state, and McKinley's secretary of state.

Those closest to McKinley, however, were delighted with his progress. Callers left the Milburn house looking happy. The New York City specialist took time off to tour Niagara Falls. Mrs. McKinley even went for a drive. Americans everywhere were just as relieved. McKinley was popular, both as president and as a human being. He brought his personal qualities of patience, tact, and kindness to his presidency. And he was quick to sense and respond to what the public wanted.

Although McKinley had tried to avoid war during his

first term, the situation had spiraled out of control. Cuban rebels were fighting Spain for their independence, and most Americans supported their struggle. Then an American battleship, the *Maine*, blew up in Cuban waters, killing 260 American sailors. Although the cause of the explosion was never determined, the press inflamed the public into believing that Spain was responsible. On April 25, 1898, the United States declared war against Spain. Four months later, the United States won the Spanish-American War and the nation optimistically entered the twentieth century as a new world power.

Americans were also optimistic about the president's recovery. On the sixth day after the shooting, McKinley ate solid food. But that night he was in agony. The doctors treated him for indigestion.

It wasn't indigestion. It was gangrene and a critical infection. Whether or not placing a drain in the wound would have saved the president's life can't be answered. However, President McKinley, who was overweight and had never been known to exercise, had no strength or physical reserves to draw on. As rain, thunder, and lightning raged overhead, his weakened heart began to fail. By dawn, he was near death.

"It is useless, gentlemen," he told the doctors. "I think we ought to have prayer." He asked for his wife.

Ida McKinley held her husband's hand and kissed him. He put his arm around her and smiled. "Good-bye—good-bye, all," he said. "It is God's way. His will, not ours, be done." He whispered a verse from the hymn, "Nearer My

God to Thee." Although McKinley continued to hold his wife's hand, he never spoke again.

The harsh wheeze of the president's breathing filled the room. At 2:15 A.M. on September 14, 1901, McKinley's labored breathing stopped. "The president is dead," Dr. Rixey announced. Although doctors performed an autopsy, they never found the bullet.

After her husband's death, Ida McKinley showed a strength and determination that amazed everyone. She traveled with the coffin to Washington, where William McKinley's body lay in state, first in the White House East Room and then in the Capitol rotunda. After the state funeral in the rotunda, Mrs. McKinley accompanied her husband's body back to Canton, Ohio, for burial.

President McKinley's formal funeral ceremonies began in Buffalo.

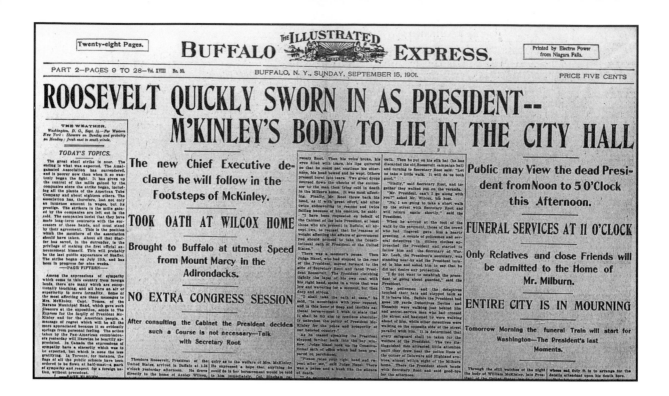

Newspaper headlines told the story.

After reports of the president's last words were made public, "Nearer My God to Thee" echoed in churches across the country. When McKinley was buried in the family vault at 3:30 P.M. on September 19, 1901, all traffic and businesses across the country stopped for five minutes. William McKinley's strong faith, simplicity, and love for the people had rarely been seen in the White House. The nation mourned his death with genuine sorrow.

THE ANARCHIST

"I killed President McKinley because I done my duty," Leon F. Czolgosz told the police after his arrest. "I saw a great many people there saluting him, bowing to him, paying homage to him, and honoring the President."

Twenty-eight-year-old Czolgosz was a slightly built, rather handsome young man with large vacant eyes. The child of poor Polish immigrant parents, he was withdrawn, timid, and humorless.

After a few years of schooling, Czolgosz worked at low-paying factory jobs. In his spare time, he read radical anarchist magazines and newspapers. Increasingly, he came to believe that all rulers and governments were the enemy of the working people.

When he was twenty-five, Czolgosz had a physical and mental breakdown. He returned to his family's Ohio farm and never worked again. For three years he isolated himself at the farm, keeping to his room and reading anarchist publications. Although he approached anarchist groups several times about joining, his knowledge of anarchism was so vague that no anarchist organization would accept him.

On August 31, 1901, Czolgosz traveled to Buffalo where he bought a .32 caliber revolver. He heard the president's speech at the Pan-American Exposition on September 5. The next morning he followed McKinley to Niagara Falls.

That afternoon Czolgosz lined up early at the Temple of Music. As he stood in line, he took the gun from his pocket. Gripping it, he wrapped a handkerchief around both his hand and the gun like a bandage. Czolgosz knew that he wouldn't escape and he didn't care. "I expected after I shot him that I would be catched at it," he said later. "I didn't believe one man should have so much service and another man should have none."

Because anarchists of the time had committed a number of violent crimes, they were viewed with suspicion.

Vol XLV No 2337   IO Cents a Copy

HARPER'S WEEKLY

A JOURNAL OF CIVILIZATION

NEW YORK   OCTOBER 5, 1901

UNITED STATES

"NO ROOM ON THIS SHIP"

After President McKinley's death, public feeling ran high against all anarchists.

When Czolgosz described himself as an anarchist, authorities immediately suspected a conspiracy. All over the country anarchists were arrested and jailed. Hundreds were questioned. Some were even mobbed on the street.

Anarchists finally convinced the police that Czolgosz had never been a member of any anarchist group. A notice in an official publication five days before the shooting helped prove their case. The notice warned anarchists to avoid a man described as a dangerous crank. Although no name was mentioned, the man was clearly Czolgosz.

On September 23, Czolgosz went on trial in Buffalo. Because he didn't believe in the American judicial system, he wouldn't talk to lawyers or take the stand in his own defense. At the time, a defendant was considered sane unless he could be proven insane. Although Czolgosz was clearly insane, his lawyers never presented evidence to prove it.

After a trial that lasted only eight and a half hours, the jury brought in a verdict of guilty. Leon Czolgosz heard the death sentence without a flicker of emotion. Just before he died in the electric chair on October 29, 1901, he declared: "I killed the President because he was the enemy of the people, the good working people. I am not sorry for my crime."

THE SQUARE DEAL PRESIDENT

For more than thirteen hours the country was without a president. Vice-President Theodore Roosevelt was climbing in the Adirondack Mountains when news came that McKinley was dying. After scrambling down the mountain, he rode three relays of horse-drawn wagons to a railroad station where a special train took him to Buffalo. When he was sworn in at 3:35 P.M. on September 14, 1901, forty-two-year-old Theodore Roosevelt became the nation's youngest president.

"It shall be my aim to continue, absolutely unbroken,

the policy of President McKinley for the peace, prosperity, and the honor of our beloved country," Roosevelt pledged in his first public statement as twenty-sixth president of the United States.

Actually, all Theodore Roosevelt and William McKinley had in common was that they were both Republicans. McKinley's approach was to act after he learned what the public wanted, while Roosevelt plunged into the presidency with goals already set. Calling his programs the Square Deal, Roosevelt's aim was to make sure "that every man has a square deal."

In response to the national outcry against anarchists, Roosevelt pushed through the Federal Anti-Anarchist law. Any person who was opposed to organized government wouldn't be allowed to enter the United States.

Roosevelt then went on to steer bills through Congress

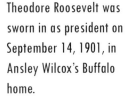

Theodore Roosevelt was sworn in as president on September 14, 1901, in Ansley Wilcox's Buffalo home.

that regulated big businesses and gave the government broader control over the railroads. Millions of acres of land were set aside for public use. A Pure Food and Drug Act protected Americans from unsafe food, medicines, and liquor. Inspection of stockyards and meat-packing houses became law.

Roosevelt's foreign policies were just as dramatic. He engineered the Panamanian revolution and then signed a treaty with Panama to build a canal linking the Atlantic and Pacific oceans. He stepped in to settle disputes between belligerent nations. To demonstrate American military power, he sent sixteen battleships on a year-and-a-half cruise around the world.

Theodore Roosevelt was elected to another term of office in November 1904. Although some Americans were unhappy with his aggressive policies, Roosevelt stirred the winds of change that improved millions of American lives.

CHANGING TIMES

William McKinley's presidency served as a bridge between the past and the future. As a businessman's president, McKinley had strong ties to the nineteenth century. He maintained gold as the standard for American currency. He supported high tariffs to keep cheap foreign goods out of the country. He opposed government regulation of businesses, costly government spending, and high taxes.

On the other hand, McKinley's foreign policies looked toward the twentieth century. Under McKinley the United

States became a world power. After the Spanish-American War, Spain turned over the Philippines, Puerto Rico, and Guam to the United States. Hawaii was annexed, Wake Island was formally occupied, and trade with China was opened.

But McKinley never understood that technical advances, improved transportation, and communication systems were changing the world. And despite America's prosperity, workers labored long hours in poorly paid jobs. Living conditions in cities were overcrowded and unhealthy. Giant corporations controlled prices and crushed unions. Natural resources were being exhausted.

William McKinley made a start at leading the country into modern times. But it would take dynamic, strong-willed Theodore Roosevelt to reform abuses and shape the presidency as it is known today.

NOVEMBER 22, 1963

Early on a gray and drizzly November 22, the president and First Lady were joined in their hotel room by several aides. One of the aides arrived with a local newspaper opened to a full-page ad. The ad not only accused the president of being soft on Communism, but it was also bordered in black like a death notice. After glancing at the ad, the president handed the newspaper to his wife. When she saw the black border, she was horrified.

"Oh, you know, we're headed into nut country today," the president said lightly, trying to defuse her alarm with humor. "You know, last night would have been a hell of a night to assassinate a president. There was the rain, and the night, and we were all getting jostled. Suppose a man had a pistol in a briefcase." With exaggerated gestures, the president cocked an imaginary pistol, whirled around, crouched low, and fired. "Then he could have dropped the gun and the briefcase and melted away in the crowd."

As soon as the president heard the laughter that he had hoped for, he got down to business. He had a full day ahead. He had agreed to give a brief talk in the hotel parking lot, followed by a speech at a breakfast meeting. He and his party would then board Air Force One for a short flight to their next destination, Dallas.

THE ETERNAL FLAME

JOHN FITZGERALD KENNEDY

May 29, 1917–November 22, 1963
Thirty-fifth President, 1961–1963

DEALEY PLAZA

Air Force One landed at Love Field in Dallas at 11:38 A.M. on Friday, November 22, 1963. Dallas officials welcomed President John Fitzgerald Kennedy and presented a bouquet of red roses to Mrs. Kennedy. From behind a fence, a waiting crowd called greetings. Urging his wife to join him, Kennedy strode over to the fence and began to shake hands. The hand-shaking didn't last long. With a tight schedule to follow, Kennedy's aides were anxious to start the presidential motorcade that would wind through downtown Dallas.

The president's 1961 Lincoln convertible had been flown in from Washington. Kennedy took the right rear seat with his wife on his left and the bouquet of roses between them. Texas Governor and Mrs. John Connally sat in the jump seat. Secret Service agents Roy Kellerman and the driver, William Greer, rode in front.

The drizzle had ended, the sun had come out, and the Lincoln's plastic bubble top was off. The president had such good luck with weather that his staff called a warm,

A smiling President and Mrs. Kennedy arrived in Dallas on Air Force One.

sunny day like this "Kennedy weather." Although Mrs. Kennedy and Mrs. Connally worried that the open car would ruin their hairdos, the president was delighted. He wanted face-to-face contact with as many people as possible.

The Dallas police chief drove the lead car. The Lincoln was next. Because Kennedy had refused to have Secret Service agents surrounding the Lincoln, four motorcycle police flanked the rear fender. Vice-President and Mrs. Lyndon Johnson, officials, staff, and press followed in a long line of cars and buses.

Everyone was astounded by the huge turnout along the eleven-mile route, perhaps as many as 250,000 people. Mrs. Kennedy, whose beauty and style were legendary, was a star attraction. This was her first vote-getting trip since her husband became president, and Kennedy was anxious for everything to go smoothly.

Certainly everything hadn't gone smoothly for John Kennedy's first one thousand days in office. At the time of his inauguration on January 20, 1961, Communism was a worldwide threat. And Communist Cuba was only ninety miles from Florida. Three months after Kennedy became president, he gave the go-ahead for CIA-trained Cuban exiles to invade Cuba and overthrow Cuba's dictator, Fidel Castro. But Castro's forces wiped out the exile force in a humiliating defeat for Kennedy and the United States.

The following year, Kennedy learned that Communist Russia was building offensive missile sites in Cuba. In a daring move, he announced a naval blockade of all Russian ships carrying military equipment to Cuba. This time the humiliating defeat was the Russians'. Backing off, they removed all their missiles from Cuba.

Kennedy admitted that his "problems are more difficult than I had imagined they were." And South Vietnam was one of the most difficult. North Vietnamese Communists were fighting to take over South Vietnam. When Kennedy came to office fewer than seven hundred American military advisors were in South Vietnam. During his presidency, that military presence was increased to almost seventeen thousand.

Right now, however, Kennedy's most pressing problem was Texas. This two-day, five-city trip to Texas was strictly political. Democratic President Kennedy had come to heal a feud among Texas Democrats as well as gain Texan support for his re-election in 1964. The stops at San Antonio, Houston, and Fort Worth had gone well. The next stop would be Austin. From there, Kennedy and his party would be guests at Vice-President Lyndon Johnson's Texas ranch for a well-earned rest.

As the Lincoln moved slowly through the crowded streets, Mrs. Kennedy slipped on her large sunglasses. Kennedy objected to the way dark glasses masked her face. Besides, he was proud of his lovely wife and aware that people were eager to see her. She was a political asset and he knew it.

"Take off your glasses, Jackie," he directed. Moments later, she put them back on without thinking. Again the president asked her to take them off.

Just before 12:30 P.M., the lead police car made a sharp left turn into Dealey Plaza and drove past the Texas School Book Depository. The Lincoln followed. The crowds had thinned out and the Kennedys and Connallys began to relax. Mrs. Connally swung around in her seat. "Mr. President, you can't say that Dallas doesn't love you," she said with a smile.

"No, you certainly can't," he replied.

Suddenly there was an explosion. Flocks of pigeons took off into the blue sky with a noisy beating of wings. As the blast of sound echoed and re-echoed in the open space of Dealey Plaza, it was hard to tell if there had been one explosion or two.

Was it a firecracker? A backfire? Although most people were puzzled, any hunters in the motorcade knew right away that a high-powered rifle had been fired. The president had been hit! A bullet had struck the back of his neck and torn through his windpipe.

Governor Connally had been hit, too. "No, no, no, no, no!" he shrieked as blood soaked his shirt. "They're going to kill us both!"

Mrs. Kennedy turned toward her husband. He was raising his hands to his throat, a dazed expression on his face,

President Kennedy was delighted with the large turnout as he and his wife rode through Dallas in their open car.

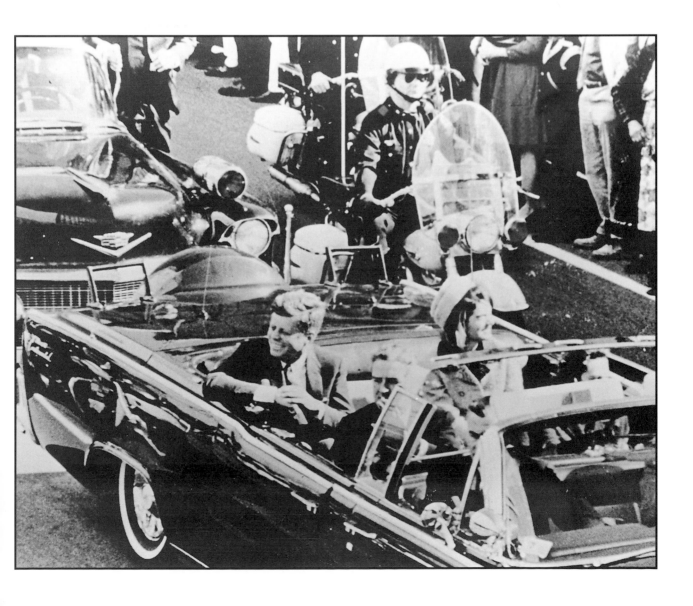

when another shot rang out. This time the bullet tore open the president's head and shattered his skull. Immediately, the Lincoln was filled with blood.

"My God, what are they doing? My God, they've killed Jack, they've killed my husband. Jack, Jack!" Mrs. Kennedy screamed. She jumped out of her seat and scrambled up onto the trunk of the still-moving Lincoln.

Agent Clint Hill, who was riding in the follow-up Secret Service car, was the first to react. He leapt out and ran toward the Lincoln. Mrs. Kennedy was crawling along the trunk on her hands and knees. Hill grabbed a hand-hold, pulled himself up, and pushed her to safety in the back seat.

"Move it out!" Agent Kellerman yelled at Greer. He then radioed the lead car. "We are hit. Get us to a hospital."

As the Lincoln sped toward Parkland Hospital, Mrs. Kennedy held her husband in her arms. "He's dead—they've killed him—oh, oh Jack, oh Jack, I love you," she repeated over and over.

When the Lincoln arrived at Parkland Hospital, Mrs. Kennedy refused to let anyone take her husband from her. Agent Clint Hill realized that she didn't want people to see the president's devastating wound. He took off his jacket and gently covered the president's head. Only then did Jackie Kennedy release her husband.

With Mrs. Kennedy present in the trauma room, eleven Parkland Hospital doctors tried to revive the mortally injured president. At 1 P.M., the surgeon in charge turned to Mrs. Kennedy. "Your husband has sustained a fatal wound," he told her.

After two Roman Catholic priests administered the last rites, the president's body was laid in a coffin. Mrs. Kennedy sat beside the coffin in a high-speed drive by ambulance to Love Field and Air Force One. But the take-off for Washington was delayed until Vice-President Lyndon Johnson could be sworn in as president.

Federal District Judge Sarah Hughes, the first woman to administer the presidential oath of office, boarded Air Force One. Johnson asked his wife to stand on his right and Mrs. Kennedy on his left. At 2:28 P.M., Judge Hughes swore in Lyndon Baines Johnson as the thirty-sixth president of the United States. Minutes later the plane was airborne.

Air Force One left behind a city in turmoil. The Secret Service called Dallas a "hot" city. Ultra-conservative political groups violently opposed President Kennedy's liberal policies. The day before Kennedy's arrival in Dallas, "Wanted for Treason" posters with mug shots of the president had been distributed all over the city.

No one had been happy about the president's trip to Dallas. UN Ambassador Adlai Stevenson had recently been the object of a Dallas mob's fury. He had been spit on and hit over the head with a picket sign. Senator William Fulbright, who knew Dallas well, had pleaded with Kennedy not to go. Even Texas Governor Connally had wanted Kennedy to reconsider his Dallas stop.

But Kennedy ignored all the warnings. "If anyone wanted to kill you, you wouldn't be around," he commented. He was casual, too, about the fact that the last six presidents who had been elected in a year ending in zero had died in office.

As Air Force One touched down at Andrews Air Force

WANTED

FOR

TREASON

THIS MAN is wanted for treasonous activities against the United States:

1. Betraying the Constitution (which he swore to uphold):
He is turning the sovereignty of the U. S. over to the communist controlled United Nations.
He is betraying our friends (Cuba, Katanga, Portugal) and befriending our enemies (Russia, Yugoslavia, Poland).
2. He has been WRONG on innumerable issues affecting the security of the U.S. (United Nations-Berlin wall-Missle removal-Cuba-Wheat deals-Test Ban Treaty, etc.)
3. He has been lax in enforcing Communist Registration laws.
4. He has given support and encouragement to the Communist inspired racial riots.
5. He has illegally invaded a sovereign State with federal troops.
6. He has consistantly appointed Anti-Christians to Federal office: Upholds the Supreme Court in its Anti-Christian rulings.
Aliens and known Communists abound in Federal offices.
7. He has been caught in fantastic LIES to the American people (including personal ones like his previous marraige and divorce).

1514

A sinister handbill was circulated in Dallas before President Kennedy's arrival.

Base, Maryland, it carried the body of John F. Kennedy, who had been elected in a zero year, 1960. Under the glare of floodlights, the coffin was lowered from the plane into a waiting ambulance.

Ever since the shooting, Mrs. Kennedy had refused to change her clothes. "Let them see what they did to him," she insisted.

When TV cameras focused on Jackie Kennedy as she followed her husband's coffin into the ambulance, the world did see. The sight of her stained and bloody suit and stockings shocked TV viewers. After three years of watching the Kennedys, Americans had become accustomed to the glamorous First Lady's elegantly groomed image.

In 1947 Jacqueline Lee Bouvier had been dubbed Queen Deb [Debutante] of the Year. Like her husband, she came from wealth and privilege. But unlike her husband, she had no interest in politics. She preferred the quiet world of books, music, art, and the theater. Horses and horseback riding had been her passion since childhood.

Jack Kennedy, on the other hand, grew up in a fiercely competitive family whose passions were politics, sailing, and contact sports. His father's motto was "Second best is a loser." Despite their differences, the handsome young couple fell in love and were married in a fashionable Newport, Rhode Island, wedding on September 12, 1953.

With such contrasting interests, the Kennedys' marriage was often rocky. Separation had even been discussed. Both Kennedys, however, were devoted to their children, Caroline and John, Jr. And they were both brokenhearted when their third child died shortly after birth in August 1963, just three months before John Kennedy's own death.

Rain on Saturday, November 23, mirrored the nation's tears. After an autopsy that began Friday night and lasted into Saturday morning, the president's coffin was closed at Mrs. Kennedy's request. Covered by an American flag, it was placed on a catafalque in the East Room. After a private funeral mass, government leaders, statesmen, and diplomats arrived at the White House to pay their last respects.

Saturday's dreary rain ended and Sunday dawned a "Kennedy weather" day, clear and brisk, with sunny skies. At 1 P.M., Mrs. Kennedy appeared on the White House portico with her two children for the procession of her husband's coffin to the Capitol. In his inaugural address, President Kennedy had said that "the torch has been passed to a new generation of Americans." Now the sight of the young family on America's TV screens was a touching reminder that Kennedy had not only been president, but also a youthful husband and father.

John F. Kennedy was born on May 29, 1917, to Boston-Irish parents, the second of nine children. He was a sickly child who spent long stretches of time in bed, in school infirmaries, or in hospitals. After a private school education, he graduated from Harvard in 1940.

During World War II, Kennedy served in the Navy. In August 1943, a Japanese destroyer rammed and sank the PT boat that he commanded. Kennedy's quick thinking saved his men, all but two crewmen who had been killed instantly. Although his action earned him a medal, it also worsened an old back injury and Kennedy was sent home for surgery.

In 1946 Kennedy ran for the House of Representatives as the Democratic candidate from Massachusetts. He served in the House until he was elected to the Senate in 1952. Although Kennedy had two more back operations in 1954 and 1955, they were unsuccessful and he lived with chronic back pain. He also suffered from Addison's disease, an adrenal gland deficiency, which required daily cortisone treatment.

Although no Roman Catholic had ever been elected president, Roman Catholic John Kennedy became the Democratic candidate in 1960. He defeated Richard Nixon by the narrowest popular-vote margin in the twentieth century. At forty-three, he was the youngest man ever to be elected president.

Americans may have divided their loyalties in the voting booth, but they were united in their grief. Weeping spectators lined Washington's Pennsylvania Avenue as a military honor guard and riderless horse accompanied John Kennedy's coffin from the White House to the Capitol. The flag-draped coffin was strapped to the gun carriage that had carried President Franklin Roosevelt's coffin in 1945.

In the Capitol rotunda, President Kennedy's coffin rested on the catafalque on which Abraham Lincoln's coffin had rested. After a brief ceremony, hundreds of thousands of Americans expressed their sorrow by silently walking past the closed coffin.

On Monday, November 25, the coffin was formally escorted back to the White House to the roll of muffled drums. From there, Mrs. Kennedy, family members, and two hundred world leaders walked behind the coffin to St. Matthew's Cathedral for the state funeral mass. After the service, Mrs. Kennedy, Caroline, who would have her sixth birthday two days later, and John, who was three that day, paused on the cathedral steps.

"John, you can salute Daddy now and say good-bye to him," Mrs. Kennedy whispered to her son as the coffin was carried out. The boy, who had been called John-John by his father, saluted the coffin in a gesture that brought the country to its knees.

By Monday afternoon, the ceremonies were drawing to a close. From St. Matthew's Cathedral, the funeral motorcade drove to the National Cemetery in Arlington, Virginia, for the burial service. After a fighter jet flyover, prayers, a twenty-one gun salute, and "Taps," the American flag was removed from John F. Kennedy's coffin, folded, and presented to his widow.

After President Kennedy's funeral service, John, Jr., gave his father a farewell salute.

Still holding the flag, Mrs. Kennedy approached the grave site with a burning taper. She touched the taper to a torch installed in the ground and the eternal flame sprang to life. As the mourners left the cemetery, the torch that had been passed to a new generation of Americans burned brightly.

THE MARXIST

Moments after the shooting in Dealey Plaza, an eyewitness gave Dallas police the description of a man he had seen in the sixth-floor window of the Texas School Book Depository. A short time later, police officer J. D. Tippit spotted a young man on the street who fit the description. But when Tippit stopped the suspect for questioning, the young man shot and killed him. With the help of witnesses, the Dallas police captured the gunman in a darkened movie theater where he had fled.

"Everyone will know who I am now," Lee Harvey Oswald boasted after his arrest.

Oswald was a twenty-four-year-old loner with a ninth-grade education. At the age of seventeen, he had enlisted in the Marines. Court-martialed twice, Oswald dropped out of the Marines after three years. Silent, moody, and quick to anger, he drifted from one unskilled job to another.

Oswald had showed an early interest in Karl Marx and Marxism. As the founder of the theories of Communism, Marx believed that if differences of class and rank were wiped out, and the government owned all property, everyone would be equal. In 1959 Oswald traveled to the Soviet Union, where he tried unsuccessfully to give up his American citizenship at the United States Embassy. When he was asked by an embassy staff member why he wanted to renounce his citizenship, he replied, "I am a Marxist."

In 1961 Oswald met and married a young Russian woman. But Oswald was just as unhappy in the Soviet Union as he had been in the United States. The following year he left the Soviet Union with his wife and infant daughter to settle in Texas, first in Fort Worth and then in Dallas.

Turning his attention to Communist Cuba, Oswald next worked briefly for the Fair Play for Cuba Committee. Nevertheless, Cuban authorities refused to issue him a visa to visit Cuba. In October 1963 Oswald took a low-paying job at the Texas School Book Depository. A few days later, Oswald's wife, who had recently left him, gave birth to their second daughter.

On November 23, 1963, Oswald was charged with the assassination of President John F. Kennedy and the murder of Officer J. D. Tippit. The next day television cameras followed Oswald as police escorted him through the prison basement for transfer to another jail. Millions of TV viewers were stunned to see a man dart forward and fire a pistol point-blank at Oswald. The man was Jack Ruby, a Dallas nightclub owner.

"You killed the President, you rat!" Ruby shouted.

Oswald collapsed, his face contorted with pain. He was pronounced dead at Parkland Hospital less than two hours later.

With Oswald's death, countless questions about

As Lee Harvey Oswald was led through the prison basement, Jack Ruby shot him.

Kennedy's death were left unanswered. President Lyndon Johnson appointed a commission to investigate the assassination under the leadership of Supreme Court Chief

Justice Earl Warren. Ten months later, the Warren Commission stated: "The shots which killed President Kennedy and wounded Governor Connally were fired by Lee Harvey Oswald."

Millions of Americans were unhappy with the Warren Report's "lone assassin" verdict. Governor Connally, who had recovered from his wounds, and other eyewitnesses, disagreed on almost every detail. They differed on how many shots had been fired and which direction they had come from. There was even disagreement about which bullet had struck Kennedy and which had struck Connally.

In 1977 the House of Representatives reopened the investigation. Two years later, the House Select Committee on Assassinations concluded that Kennedy "was probably killed as the result of a conspiracy." But the committee admitted that it "was unable to identify the other gunman or the extent of the conspiracy."

If there was a conspiracy, who was behind it? Over the years almost every level of government, both the right and the left, have been implicated. The FBI, the CIA, the Secret Service, and the military establishment have come under suspicion. So have organized crime, the Dallas police, the big business community, the Soviet intelligence agency, the Vietnamese connection, anti-Castro Cuban exiles, and pro-Castro Cubans.

In 1994 Congress appointed a federal Assassination Review Board to gather records about Kennedy's assassination and make them public. But to this day, no one theory has ever satisfied the American people. The true story may never be known. Or, if it becomes known, it may not be believed. All that is certain is that debate, argument, and controversy are bound to continue.

THE GREAT SOCIETY PRESIDENT

When Lyndon Baines Johnson came to the presidency, he was already an experienced politician. Born near Stonewall, Texas, Johnson had been elected to the United States House of Representatives at the age of twenty-eight. Eleven years later he was elected to the Senate. With boundless drive, energy, and ambition, he became Senate Democratic Minority Leader in 1953 and Majority Leader in 1955. After wielding so much power, it came as a surprise to just about everyone when Johnson agreed to be Kennedy's vice-presidential running mate in the 1960 election.

After being sworn in as president on November 22, 1963,

With his wife and Mrs. Kennedy at his side, Lyndon Johnson took the presidential oath of office in the crowded cabin of Air Force One, November 22, 1963.

Johnson immediately pledged support for the social programs that Kennedy hadn't been able to get through Congress. Johnson's goal was to create what he called a Great Society that would better all American lives. In his first year he masterminded the Civil Rights Act of 1964, a tax cut, federal aid to transportation, anti-poverty projects, and establishment of the Job Corps.

"They say that Jack Kennedy had style but I'm the one who got the bills passed," Johnson pointed out to critics who compared his sometimes heavy-handed but effective tactics unfavorably with Kennedy's cool and intellectual approach.

Although Johnson committed more and more American troops and more and more money to South Vietnam, he ran for president in 1964 as the peace candidate. "We don't want our American boys to do the fighting for Asian boys," he stated.

Johnson won the election by a huge margin. His overwhelming victory enabled him to push more Great Society programs through Congress: Medicare for the elderly, the Voting Rights Act of 1965, federal aid to schools, low-cost housing, and conservation measures.

But shortly after his second term began, Johnson reversed his stand on America's role in South Vietnam. "We will not surrender and we will not retreat," he declared. Before the end of 1965, he had sent 165,000 American troops to fight in the Vietnam War. A year and a half later, that number stood at 460,000 with eleven thousand American lives lost.

Loyal Americans marched in protest of the war. Other loyal Americans urged Johnson to win the war at any cost. The country was being pulled apart and Johnson knew it. In March 1968 he announced that he would not run for another term as president.

Johnson's Great Society achievements in civil rights, care for the elderly, and the war on poverty had been the most sweeping since the 1930s. But his escalation of the Vietnam War ended his long political career. Lyndon B. Johnson died of a heart attack at his Texas ranch on January 22, 1973.

ON CAMERA

John Fitzgerald Kennedy was the first president to be defined by television. As the 1960 Democratic candidate, he and the Republican candidate, Richard Nixon, held televised debates. In contrast to Nixon's darkly nervous performance, Kennedy's vigor, quick wit, and good looks lit up the TV screen.

After Kennedy's assassination, TV coverage allowed grieving Americans to participate in the funeral ceremonies. Jackie Kennedy was the guiding spirit as she led the nation through the mourning process. Her courage and grace restored sanity and a sense of national pride to the country.

With Kennedy's death, no one will ever know for sure what his plans for the future might have been. Would he have escalated the Vietnam War or brought American troops home? The answer to that question will probably never be known.

What is known is that Kennedy conveyed an optimistic vision of how the country could move forward. All things seemed possible as the young and not-so-young committed themselves to bettering the lives of people around the world. John F. Kennedy's legacy was his style, humor, intelligence, and enduring sense of hopeful expectancy.

THE SURVIVORS

THE CAPITOL PORTICO

JANUARY 30, 1835

On a dreary, gray January 30, 1835, President Andrew Jackson arrived at the Capitol to attend a congressman's funeral. Seated with other government leaders, Jackson listened to a sermon about the uncertainty of life and the ever-nearness of death.

Jackson had no idea how near to death he was. At that moment, a thirty-four-year-old housepainter, Richard Lawrence, was on the Capitol's East Portico waiting for him.

Lawrence had carefully loaded two powerful pistols with lead balls and a fine quality gunpowder with the intention of assassinating Jackson. Lawrence, who had immigrated from England as a boy, believed himself to be King Richard III of Great Britain. He claimed that he was owed money for property in England that the United States government had taken from him. With Jackson dead, Lawrence was sure that Congress would pay the money due him.

President Andrew Jackson escaped injury as a deranged gunman's two pistols both misfired.

The funeral ended and the Capitol door opened. A long procession of mourners followed the congressman's coffin. Andrew Jackson, who was frail and in poor health, was far back in line. Lawrence took the pistols from his pockets, cocked them, and held one in each hand under his cloak.

As the president started across the Capitol portico, Lawrence leapt in front of him. Aiming his pistol at Jackson's heart, he fired from eight feet away. The percussion cap exploded but the gunpowder didn't ignite. The portico's stonework magnified the sound and the procession broke up in chaos. Dropping the first pistol, Lawrence transferred the other pistol to his right hand.

Instead of ducking for cover, a furious Jackson raised his cane and headed for Lawrence. The second pistol was only inches from Jackson's chest when Lawrence pulled the trigger. Incredibly, the second pistol misfired, too. The men surrounding Jackson wrestled Lawrence to the ground and seized his guns.

Jackson was still determined to give Lawrence a caning. He was certain that one of his political enemies was behind the attack. "Let me alone! Let me alone! I know where this comes from," he shouted as his companions struggled to restrain him.

Andrew Jackson was no stranger to violence. As a boy, he had been captured by the British during the American Revolution. When he had refused to clean a British officer's boots, the officer had slashed young Andy's head with a saber and cut his arm to the bone. Shot twice in a brawl, Jackson had once taken a bullet close to his heart in a duel. He had stood his ground, fired back, and mortally wounded his opponent. An Indian fighter and a soldier, Jackson was called Old Hickory by his men, who accurately described him as "tough as hickory."

Richard Lawrence was brought to trial on April 11, 1835. Francis Scott Key, who wrote the words to "The Star-Spangled Banner," was the prosecuting attorney. Even Key agreed that Lawrence was insane and not responsible for his actions. At one point, Lawrence addressed the jury. "It is for me, gentlemen, to pass judgment on you and not you upon me," he scolded.

After a day-and-a-half trial, the jury returned a not-guilty verdict by reason of insanity. Richard Lawrence spent the next twenty-six years in mental hospitals. He died in 1861, having outlived Jackson by sixteen years. To the end of his life, Andrew Jackson believed that the assassination attempt had been staged by a political enemy.

MILWAUKEE, WISCONSIN

OCTOBER 14, 1912

Several thousand people gathered outside the Hotel Gilpatrick in Milwaukee, Wisconsin, on the evening of October 14, 1912. Theodore Roosevelt was due to give a speech in a nearby auditorium and the waiting crowd knew that he would be coming out soon.

Former Vice-President Theodore Roosevelt had been sworn in as president after William McKinley's assassination in 1901. Although Roosevelt was elected to serve another term in 1904, he decided not to run again in 1908. His good friend, William Howard Taft, became the Republican candidate and was elected. But Roosevelt grew unhappy with Taft's policies. In 1912 Roosevelt announced that he would run for president against Taft, this time as the candidate of the Progressive, or Bull Moose, Party.

Colonel Roosevelt, as he liked to be called, had been campaigning around the country for two months. Thirty-six-year-old John Schrank had been secretly stalking him through eight states. Schrank was violently opposed to any president serving three terms, and he was especially opposed to Roosevelt. On September 15, 1901, the night after McKinley's death, Schrank had dreamed that McKinley sat up in his coffin and blamed Theodore Roosevelt for his murder.

Schrank had a second vision in 1912 after Roosevelt became a candidate. According to Schrank, on September 15, 1912, McKinley had again appeared to him. "Let not a murderer take the presidential chair," McKinley had said.

Now the short, plump, and neatly dressed Schrank waited outside the Hotel Gilpatrick near Roosevelt's car. In his pocket he carried a loaded .38 caliber Colt revolver. At 8 P.M., Colonel Roosevelt came out of the hotel. He walked briskly to his open car, climbed in, and waved to the cheering bystanders. Schrank poked his gun between the two men in front of him and pulled the trigger. Roosevelt staggered back as a flash of heat filled his chest. The bullet had struck him in the right breast and fractured his fourth rib. Before Schrank could fire again, Roosevelt's stenographer, an ex-football player, tackled him to the sidewalk.

Hotheads in the crowd yelled: "Lynch him!"

Colonel Roosevelt called out: "Don't hurt him. Bring him here. I want to look at him."

When Schrank was brought over to the car, Roosevelt studied him intently and then asked him why he had done it. Before Schrank could answer, Roosevelt told the police to take him away.

Colonel Roosevelt then coughed into his hand. When he didn't see blood, he knew that the bullet hadn't punctured his lungs. Luckily, the bullet had struck his breast pocket, which held a fifty-page folded copy of his speech and a metal eyeglass case. The contents of his pocket had saved his life.

Although Roosevelt's companions begged him to go to a hospital, he refused. All his life, Theodore Roosevelt had fought against any kind of physical weakness and he

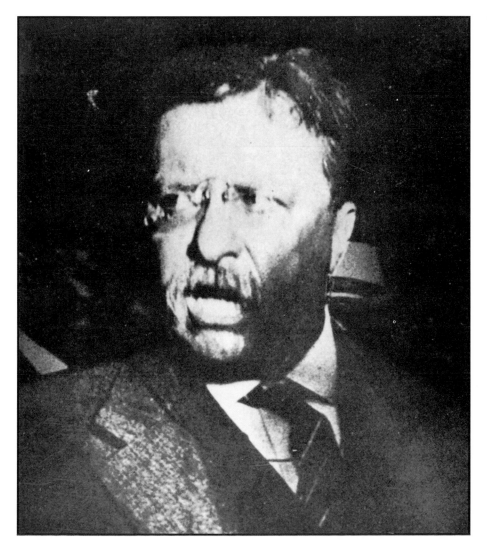

Theodore Roosevelt was photographed moments after being shot.

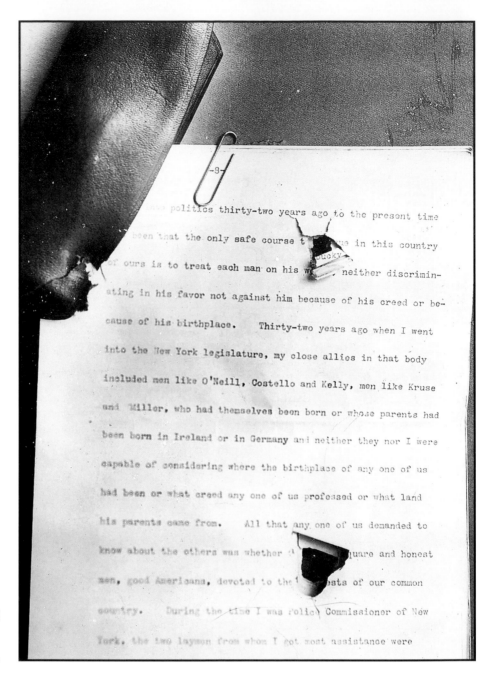

wouldn't give in now. But his shirt and trousers were bloody, and his left shoe was filled with blood by the time he reached the auditorium.

"It takes more than one bullet to kill a Bull Moose," Roosevelt told his astonished audience.

Despite suffering from shock and loss of blood, Colonel Roosevelt spoke for fifty minutes. When he was finished, it was decided that he should be treated in a Chicago hospital by a specialist. Roosevelt boarded his private railroad car, went to bed, and slept. On his arrival in Chicago at 3:30 A.M. he was rushed to the hospital where he remained for six days.

Although Schrank was charged with armed assault with intent to kill, he was never brought to trial. Five experts testified that Schrank was "suffering from insane delusions...in our opinion he is insane at the present time." John Schrank spent the rest of his life in mental hospitals. He died on September 15, 1943, the anniversary of his two visitations from McKinley.

Theodore Roosevelt carried John Schrank's bullet in his chest until his death from natural causes in 1919.

MIAMI, FLORIDA

FEBRUARY 15, 1933

Although Franklin Delano Roosevelt was elected Democratic president in November 1932, Inauguration Day wasn't until March 4, 1933. In February, Roosevelt vacationed on a friend's yacht off the coast of Florida. Upon his return, he was scheduled to give a speech at Miami's Bay Front Park.

On the warm, balmy evening of February 15, 1933, more than ten thousand people flocked to the park's outdoor amphitheater to hear the president-elect. Giuseppe Zangara arrived early. He carried a loaded .32 caliber revolver in his pocket.

Thirty-two-year-old Zangara had always bitterly resented people who had more than he did, especially education or the opportunity to better themselves. As a young boy in Italy, his father had made him quit school and go to work. He blamed his lifelong stomach trouble on the hard labor he'd done as a child. Angry at the world, Zangara favored the assassination of all "capitalist presidents and kings."

At first Zangara, who lived in Miami, had planned to

assassinate President Herbert Hoover. But when he heard that President-elect Roosevelt was to appear in Miami, he decided that it would be more convenient to assassinate Roosevelt. He later said, "Hoover and Roosevelt—everybody the same."

Although Zangara planned to sit in the first row of the amphitheater, others had come even earlier and the front row chairs were taken. Zangara was only five feet tall. By the time he found a seat, all he could see was the back of people's heads.

Roosevelt was driven to the front of the amphitheater about 9 P.M. in an open Buick touring car. As his driver parked, Roosevelt saw an old friend, Chicago mayor Anton Cermak, seated on the bandstand.

Franklin Roosevelt, who had been paralyzed by polio twelve years before, sat on top of the Buick's back seat. Holding a portable microphone, he spoke informally. As soon as he finished, he beckoned to Mayor Cermak to join him. The two men chatted briefly.

As the crowd began to thin out, Zangara spotted an empty aisle seat only twenty feet or so from Roosevelt's car. He scrambled up on the chair, drew his pistol, and fired five rounds as fast as he could. But the chair was wobbly and Zangara's aim was unsteady. One bullet ripped into Cermak's right lung. Four other bystanders were also wounded, one in the abdomen and three in the head. Roosevelt wasn't hit at all. Enraged bystanders mobbed Zangara, who had to be rescued by police.

Although Secret Service agents tried to rush Roosevelt out of the amphitheater, they hadn't driven fifteen feet

Although five gunshots were fired soon after Franklin Roosevelt finished his speech, the president-elect was unharmed.

before Roosevelt ordered them to stop. He insisted that they take Mayor Cermak to the hospital. Roosevelt held the wounded man in his arms the whole way. "Tony, keep quiet. Don't move," he said. "It won't hurt you if you keep quiet and remain perfectly still." Although the other four victims survived, Mayor Cermak died two and a half weeks later.

On February 20, 1933, Zangara was tried on four counts of assault and the attempted assassination of the president-elect. He pleaded guilty and was sentenced to eighty years in prison. After Anton Cermak died, Zangara was tried again, this time for murder. As before, he pleaded guilty.

Judged to be sane, Giuseppe Zangara was sentenced to death. He died in the electric chair on March 20, 1933, just sixteen days after Franklin Delano Roosevelt was sworn in as the thirty-second president of the United States.

BLAIR HOUSE

NOVEMBER 1, 1950

While work was being done on the White House, President Harry S. Truman and his family lived across Pennsylvania Avenue in Blair House. After lunch on an unusually warm November 1, 1950, President Truman went up to his bedroom to take a nap. At 2:15 P.M., two Puerto Rican men approached Blair House from opposite directions. Twenty-five-year-old Griselio Torresola was armed with a German Luger. Thirty-six-year-old Oscar Collazo carried a German Walther P-38 automatic pistol. Between them they packed sixty-nine rounds of ammunition.

Fanatical members of the Puerto Rican Nationalist Party, Torresola and Collazo planned to assassinate President Truman to draw attention to their cause. They were willing to sacrifice their own lives to gain independence for Puerto Rico, which had been a United States possession since the 1898 Spanish-American War.

Ironically, President Truman had done more for Puerto Rico than any other president. He had backed a liberal form of government for Puerto Rico, appointed the first

Puerto Rican native as governor, and extended Social Security to Puerto Ricans.

Outside Blair House, White House Police stood guard. Private Donald Birdzell's post was by the front steps. Private Leslie Coffelt was stationed in a sentry booth west of the front door. Private Joseph Davidson was in the east sentry booth chatting with Secret Service agent Floyd Boring. Private Joseph Downs had just finished his watch and was headed for the basement door.

All of a sudden, Private Birdzell heard the metallic click of a gun misfiring. He looked up to see Collazo eight feet away aiming a pistol at him. As Private Birdzell drew his own gun, Collazo fired again. The bullet struck Birdzell's right leg. Birdzell hobbled out into Pennsylvania Avenue to draw gunfire away from the president. Although Collazo shot Birdzell again, Birdzell returned his fire.

At the same time, Torresola had approached the west sentry booth. He fired three times point-blank at Private Coffelt, who fell in a pool of blood. Torresola next hit Private Downs with three more rounds. Torresola then turned his gun on Private Birdzell, who was lying in the street, and shot him in the left leg. Wounded in both legs, Birdzell braced his gun on the pavement and fired back. From his sentry booth, the dying Private Coffelt drew his gun and shot Torresola in the head, killing him instantly.

From the east booth, Private Davidson and Secret Service agent Boring fired at Collazo. Two shots nicked him. The third shot struck him in the chest and he went down.

With both assassins felled, the gun battle was over. Twenty-seven rounds had been fired in less than three minutes. Awakened by the shooting, President Truman suddenly appeared at his bedroom window.

"Get back! Get back!" Agent Boring yelled. Truman quickly moved out of sight.

Private Coffelt died less than four hours later. Private Birdzell and Private Downs survived their wounds, as did Oscar Collazo.

With Torresola dead, only Collazo was brought to trial. Convicted on four counts, including murder, he was sentenced to death.

In an act of compassion and a goodwill gesture toward Puerto Rico, which had no death penalty, President

President Harry Truman calmly dedicated a statue in Arlington National Cemetery less than an hour after an assassination attempt was made on his life.

Truman reduced Collazo's death sentence to life imprisonment. In 1979 President Jimmy Carter freed Collazo. Returning to Puerto Rico, Collazo was greeted as a hero by the small band of Nationalists still left.

SACRAMENTO, CALIFORNIA

SEPTEMBER 5, 1975

President Gerald Ford was in Sacramento, California, on September 5, 1975, to discuss the problems of violent crime. After breakfast in his hotel, he walked across the capitol grounds to meet with California's governor. It was a warm and sunny morning and people were lined up behind ropes. As the president walked by they called out friendly greetings.

Ford, who was known as Mr. Nice Guy, began shaking hands. He noticed a small, slight young woman in a long red dress and red turban, who kept pace with him from behind the ropes. She looked as if she were waiting to shake his hand. But when Ford reached out, he found himself looking into the barrel of a .45 caliber pistol. Two things happened at once. Ford ducked and Secret Service agent Larry Buendorf grabbed the woman's gun.

"Don't get excited!" the young woman shouted. "It didn't go off! It didn't go off!"

Secret Service agents rushed President Gerald Ford (center) to safety following an assassination scare in Sacramento, California.

As agents seized the woman, other agents hustled the president into the capitol. Anxious to avoid a panic, Ford told them to slow down. "Everything is all right," he said quietly. At his meeting with the governor, Ford didn't even mention the assassination attempt.

Gerald Ford was back in Washington before he learned that the young woman in red was twenty-six-year-old Lynette Alice Fromme, known as Squeaky. After running away from home as a teenager, she had been picked up by a sympathetic Charles Manson and his "family." Manson, who was serving a life sentence in prison, was the leader of the cult that had killed the actress Sharon Tate and six others in 1969.

As spokeswoman for what was left of the "Manson family," Fromme was obsessed with clearing Manson's name. She viewed him as a Christ figure. By threatening the president, Fromme counted on standing trial so that Manson would be called as a witness. He would then have a platform to proclaim his message to the world. After her arrest, Fromme, whose pistol hadn't been loaded, explained: "I wasn't going to shoot him [Ford]. I just wanted to get some attention for a new trial for Charlie and the girls."

Fromme considered her own trial to be a farce. Manson was never called as a witness, and she refused to cooperate. The jury found Fromme sane and sentenced her to life imprisonment with no parole. In 1987 she escaped from the West Virginia prison where she was being held. Because of fears for Gerald Ford's safety, a nationwide alarm went out. Luckily, Fromme was found two days later only a few miles from the prison.

SAN FRANCISCO, CALIFORNIA

SEPTEMBER 22, 1975

Shrugging off the assassination attempt, President Gerald Ford was back in California seventeen days later. At 3:30 P.M., on September 22, 1975, he left San Francisco's St. Francis Hotel where he had just given a talk. Bystanders stood on either side of the hotel entrance, with three thousand or more people across the street in Union Square. Ford waved to the crowd as he headed for the limousine that would take him to the airport.

Forty-five-year-old Sara Jane Moore had been waiting three hours in Union Square for President Ford to come out. As soon as he appeared, she took a .38 caliber pistol from her purse. With the hammer already cocked, she aimed at the president, who was some forty feet away. Just as Moore pulled the trigger, an alert ex-Marine standing nearby shoved her arm to deflect her aim. The bullet passed within a few feet of Ford, hit the front of the hotel, and then ricocheted to the right. It struck a cabdriver, wounding him slightly.

When Ford heard the explosion, he flinched and clutched his chest. For a split second there was silence…followed by pandemonium. Two Secret Service agents shoved Ford down behind the limousine, opened the car door, and pushed him inside. As they piled on top of him, one of the agents yelled to the driver, "Go!"

They sped to the airport. "Hey, will you guys get off?" the president complained. "You're smothering me."

As Ford boarded Air Force One, the official White House photographer greeted him with a smile. "Other than that, Mr. President, how did you like San Francisco?" The tension eased and everyone laughed.

President Gerald Ford waved to bystanders outside a San Francisco hotel seconds before a would-be assassin's bullet barely missed him.

Sara Jane Moore, who was captured at the scene, had been raised in a middle-class West Virginia family. She had been married five times and had four children. When her last marriage failed in 1971, Moore became involved in the radical politics of the day. Shortly after she started attending left-wing meetings, the FBI approached her about becoming an informer. She agreed. But she soon felt guilty about betraying the people who had become her friends. She confided in one of them about her covert role.

As soon as Moore's radical friends found out that she was an FBI informer, they wanted nothing more to do with her. Without her left-wing contacts, Moore was useless to the FBI and they dropped her, too. She was totally isolated.

When Moore heard about Squeaky Fromme's attack on the president, she had a brainstorm. She would get back in the good graces of her friends by assassinating President Gerald Ford. Knowing that she would be caught, she considered her act to be a personal sacrifice. At her trial, Sara Jane Moore pleaded guilty to the charge of attempted assassination of the president. She was given a life sentence.

Only hours after Moore's attack on him, Gerald Ford stayed true to his Mr. Nice Guy image. "I don't think any person as president ought to cower in the face of a limited number of people who want to take the law into their own hands," he told reporters. "If we can't have that opportunity of talking with one another, seeing one another, shaking hands with one another, something has gone wrong in our society."

WASHINGTON, D.C.

MARCH 30, 1981

On a gray and rainy March 30, 1981, President Ronald Reagan strode out the back door of the Washington Hilton hotel after giving a luncheon speech. As he headed for his limousine, he noticed office workers leaning out their windows. He raised his arm and waved to them.

There was a sudden series of pops, like a string of firecrackers exploding. The president froze. Secret Service agent Jerry Parr, who immediately recognized the sound as gunshots, pushed Reagan into the back seat of the limousine and fell on top of him.

"Take off! Just take off!" Parr shouted at the driver.

Experiencing a crushing pain in his chest, Reagan yelled at Parr, "You broke my ribs."

Parr quickly checked Reagan over for wounds. When he found none, he gave the order to head for the safest destination in Washington, the White House. Moments later, Reagan began coughing up bright red blood. Parr knew right away that it was blood from the president's lungs. He barked out a new order: "Get to George Washington Hospital!"

Although Reagan insisted on walking into the emergency room, once inside, he collapsed. "I can't breathe," he gasped.

The bullet had hit the limousine and ricocheted into Reagan's left armpit, bounced off a rib, and torn into his lung. Three other men had been shot. Reagan's press secretary, James Brady, suffered a severe head wound. Secret Service agent Tim McCarthy had shielded the president with his body and taken a bullet in the chest. District of Columbia policeman Thomas Delahanty had been hit in the neck. Although all three survived, James Brady would be permanently disabled.

The doctors agreed that immediate surgery was necessary to save the president's life. Nancy Reagan insisted on seeing her husband first. Ronald Reagan had always depended on jokes and stories to get a point across or lighten up a difficult situation. Trying to reassure his wife, he quipped, "Honey, I forgot to duck."

Republican President Reagan even managed a joke in the operating room. "I hope you people are all Republicans," he said to the doctors.

"Today, we're all Republicans, Mr. President," replied the surgeon, who happened to be a liberal Democrat.

During his thirteen-day hospital stay, Reagan learned that the gunman had been overpowered moments after the shooting. Twenty-five-year-old John Hinckley, Jr., who was from a well-to-do Colorado family, had briefly attended college before drifting aimlessly around the country. While in Dallas the year before, he had bought two .22 caliber handguns known as Saturday Night Specials.

Shortly before he shot the president, Hinckley wrote a letter to the movie actress Jodie Foster. Hinckley had told Foster how much he cared for her and how he was going to shoot the president to impress her. He later called his assassination attempt "the greatest love offering in the history of the world."

Four days after his near-fatal gunshot wound, a smiling but thin President Ronald Reagan was photographed with his wife at the hospital.

At his trial, the jury found John Hinckley not guilty on grounds of insanity. Hinckley was committed to St. Elizabeth's Hospital, the same hospital where Andrew Jackson's assailant, Richard Lawrence, had lived and died more than one hundred years earlier.

Because Hinckley's shot had missed Reagan's heart by only an inch, the doctors agreed that if the president had arrived at the hospital fifteen minutes later, they probably couldn't have saved his life. Ronald Reagan, who was elected in 1980, became the first president since 1820 elected in a year ending in zero to survive his term of office.

AUTHOR'S NOTE

PROTECTION OF THE PRESIDENT

During the nineteenth century, protection of the president was an on-again, off-again matter. In 1842 John Tyler, who had witnessed the attempted assassination of Andrew Jackson, became the first president to request official protection. In response, Congress assigned four armed men wearing plainclothes to the White House. Called "doormen," they were the beginning of what would become Washington's Metropolitan Police. Until that time, a doorkeeper at the north door with firearms near at hand provided the only White House protection.

During the Civil War, security tightened, and all White House doors were guarded. Abraham Lincoln and his family were accompanied everywhere by plainclothes doormen recruited from the Metropolitan Police. On the day he was shot, Lincoln approved the creation of the Secret Service in the Treasury Department. Its duty was to pursue counterfeiters who were turning out thirty to fifty percent of all money then in circulation.

After the Civil War, every president decided for himself

whether or not he would be guarded. Even after James Garfield was assassinated in 1881, the decision was left up to the president. It wasn't until the 1898 Spanish-American War that Secret Servicemen from the Treasury Department were assigned to guard the president.

William McKinley's assassination in 1901 prompted the Secretary of the Treasury to charge the Secret Service with protecting the president officially. In 1922 the White House Police was formed to guard the White House buildings and grounds. Eight years later Congress placed the uniformed White House Police under supervision of the Secret Service to form the Secret Service as it is known today.

Over the years, Secret Service protection has expanded to include the president-elect (1913); the president's immediate family (1917); the vice-president (1951); the vice-president-elect (1962); former presidents and their wives (1965); the widow of a former president until her remarriage or death (1968); a former president's children under age sixteen (1968); major presidential and vice-presidential candidates (1968); visiting heads of state and their spouses (1971).

The assassination of John F. Kennedy in 1963 marked a turning point for the Secret Service. Within ten years the force had increased from 361 agents to 1,200, while its budget went from $7.6 million to $62.6 million. Today the Secret Service has approximately 4,600 employees and screens about 20,000 threats a year.

Although the American people want their president to be protected, they also want the president to be open and accessible. Most presidents, who still have some say over how closely they are guarded, feel the same way. In the end, no matter what extraordinary precautions the Secret Service may take, the president's safety never has been, and never can be, wholly secure.

PRINCIPAL BIBLIOGRAPHY

Brooks, Stewart M. *Our Murdered Presidents: The Medical Story.* New York: Bell Publishing Co., 1966.

Clark, James C. *American Assassins: The Darker Side of Politics.* Princeton, N. J.: Princeton University Press, 1982.

Clark, James C. *The Murder of James A. Garfield.* Jefferson, N.C.: McFarland & Company, 1993.

Crook, William. *Memories of the White House.* Boston: Little, Brown and Company, 1911.

Donald, David H. *Lincoln.* New York: Simon & Schuster, 1995.

Donovan, Robert J. *The Assassins.* New York: Harper & Brothers, Publishers, 1952.

Dorman, Michael. *The Secret Service Story.* New York: Delacorte Press, 1967.

Gould, Lewis L. *The Presidency of William McKinley.* Lawrence, Kan.: The Regents Press of Kansas, 1980.

Gray, John P. *The United States vs. Charles J. Guiteau.* Vols. I, II. New York: Arno Press, 1973.

Johns, A. Wesley. *The Man Who Shot McKinley.* South Brunswick and New York: A. S. Barnes and Company, 1970.

Knappman, Edward W., ed. and Lisa Paddock. *Great American Trials.* Detroit: Gale Research, 1994.

Leech, Margaret. *In the Days of McKinley*. New York: Harper & Brothers, Publishers, 1959.

Leech, Margaret and Harry J. Brown. *The Garfield Orbit*. New York: Harper & Row, Publishers, 1978.

Leish, Kenneth W., ed. *The American Heritage Book of the Presidents and Famous Americans*. Vols. 5, 6, 7, 8, 12. New York: American Heritage Publishing Co., 1967.

Lindop, Edmund. *Assassinations that Shook America*. New York: Franklin Watts, 1992.

McKinley, James. *Assassination in America*. New York: Harper & Row, Publishers, 1975.

Manchester, William. *The Death of a President: November 1963*. New York: Harper & Row, Publishers, 1967.

Marrs, Jim. *Crossfire: The Plot that Killed Kennedy*. New York: Carroll & Graf Publishers, 1989.

Martin, Ralph. *A Hero for our Time: An Intimate Story of the Kennedy Years*. New York: Macmillan, 1983.

O'Donnell, Kenneth P. and David F. Powers. *Johnny, We Hardly Knew Ye*. Boston: Little, Brown and Company, 1972.

Oldroyd, Osborn H. *The Assassination of Abraham Lincoln*. Washington, D. C.: O. H. Oldroyd, 1901.

Peskin, Allan. *Garfield*. Kent, Oh.: Kent State University Press, 1978.

Reeves, Richard. *President Kennedy: Profile of Power*. New York: Simon & Schuster, 1993.

Sandburg, Carl. *Abraham Lincoln: The War Years.* Vol. 4. New York: Harcourt, Brace & Company, 1939.

Seale, William. *The President's House.* Vols. I, II. Washington, D. C.: White House Historical Association, 1986.

Sifakis, Carl. *Encyclopedia of Assassinations.* New York: Facts on File. 1991.

Smith, T. Burton, M.D. "Assassination Medicine." *American Heritage* 43, no. 5 (September 1992): 116 ff.

Turner, Justin G. & Linda Levitt Turner. *Mary Todd Lincoln: Her Life and Letters.* New York: Alfred A. Knopf, 1972

ILLUSTRATION CREDITS

Buffalo and Erie County Historical Society: pages 60, 71

The Dallas Morning News: page 85

Franklin D. Roosevelt Library: page 114

Gerard R. Ford Library: pages 120, 123

Harry S. Truman Library: page 117

John F. Kennedy Library: page 82

Library of Congress: pages 18, 23, 29, 32, 38, 42, 45, 46, 51, 53, 61, 63, 64, 104

Lyndon Baines Johnson Library: page 97

National Archives & Records Administration: pages 88, 95

National Park Service: pages 22, 74

New York Public Library: page 24

Parks & History Association: page 28

Ronald Reagan Library: page 127

Theodore Roosevelt Collection-Harvard College Library: pages 109, 110

Theodore Roosevelt Inaugural Site: pages 72, 76

UPI • Corbis • Bettman: page 92

INDEX